Bichon Frise

Comprehensive Care from

Puppy to Senior

Essential facts tips and information about keeping Bichon Frisé's including; Feeding, Health, Housing, Training, Care, Grooming, Breeding and much more.

Charlotte Spencer

Published by: Pet Education Publishing
ISBN: 978-1-911348-02-3

Disclaimer and Legal Notice

The author has made every effort to ensure the accuracy of the information within this book was correct at time of publication. Whilst the author has tried to keep the information up-to-date and correct, there are no representations or warranties, express or implied, about the completeness, accuracy, reliability, suitability or availability with respect to the information, products, services, or related graphics contained in this publication for any purpose. The author does not assume and hereby disclaims any liability to any party for any loss, damage, or disruption caused by errors or omissions, whether such errors or omissions result from accident, negligence, or any other cause.

The methods described within this publication are the author's prior knowledge and/or personal thoughts and/or opinions and/or experience of the subject. They are not intended to be a definitive set of instructions for this subject. Other methods, instructions, opinions and materials may be available to accomplish the same end result. Again under no circumstance can the author/publisher accept legal responsibility or liability for any loss, damage to property and/or personal injury, arising from any error or omissions from the information contained in this publication or from failure of the reader to correctly and precisely follow any information contained within the publication.

3rd party sources/information:

The author/publisher has no control, and is therefore not responsible for the content, availability or nature of any third party websites or other publications listed herein. Access and use of information of third party websites or other publications, is at your own risk. Any website publication or the information listed within them should not be implied as an endorsement or recommendation by the author/publisher. The information provided within this publication, is strictly for educational purposes and general informational purposes only. If you wish to apply ideas contained in this publication, you are taking full responsibility for your actions. Therefore, any use of this information is at your own risk.

Additional Disclaimer and Legal Notice information:

You must not in any circumstances:

a) publish, republish, sell, license, sub-license, rent, transfer, broadcast, distribute or redistribute the publication or any part of the publication;

b) edit, modify, adapt or alter the publication or any part of the publication;

c) use of the publication or any part of the publication in any way that is unlawful or in breach of any person's legal rights under any applicable law, or in any way that is offensive, indecent, discriminatory or otherwise objectionable;

d) use of the publication or any part of the publication to compete with us, whether directly or indirectly; or

e) use the publication or any part of the publication for a commercial purpose

(1) No advice

The publication contains information about Bichon Frisé dogs. The information is not advice, and should not be treated as such. You must not rely on the information in the publication as an alternative to (legal/medical/veterinary/financial/accountancy or other relevant) advice from an appropriately qualified professional. If you have any specific questions about any (legal/medical /veterinary/financial/accountancy or other relevant) matter you should consult an appropriately qualified professional.

(2) Limited Warranties

We do not warrant or represent that the use of the publication will lead to any particular outcome or result.

(3) Limitations and exclusions of liability

We will not be liable to you in respect of any business losses, including (without limitation) loss of or damage to profits, income, revenue, use, production, anticipated savings, business, contracts, commercial opportunities or goodwill.

We will not be liable to you in respect of any loss or corruption of any data, database, hardware or software. We will not be liable to you in respect of any special, indirect or consequential loss or damage.

(4) Trademarks

Registered and unregistered trademarks or service marks in the publication are the property of their respective owners. Unless stated otherwise, we do not endorse and are not affiliated with any of the holders of any such rights and as such we cannot grant any licence to exercise such rights.

Acknowledgements

I would like to extend my sincerest thanks to my family who have always supported me in everything I do. With a special gratitude, I thank my canine friends past and present, who have taught me the true meaning of friendship, devotion and loyalty, to name but a few of their fabulous traits. Their constant love, positivity and enthusiasm for life is truly inspiring.

Author Note

If you are reading this information as an experienced dog owner, then parts will already be familiar to you. Having said that, the information is intended for everyone and I am sure that even the experienced dog person will find a lot of new facts and information.

It is not my intention to patronize the reader and to tell you how you should read a book. However, unless you are an experienced dog person and are confident enough to skip certain sections, I would highly recommend that you thoroughly read all of the contents before you begin to implement any of the instructions. You may wish to take notes as you go or re-read the book a second time noting important steps to give yourself an action plan.

Also, please note that the use of pronouns like 'his', 'him' or 'her' throughout the text, is simply for ease of reading. It is generally intended to refer to both sexes. It is not meant to indicate a preference by the author of one sex over the other.

Table of Contents

Chapter One:

Understanding Bichon Frisé Dogs

Before you can decide whether a Bichon Frisé is the right pet for you, you need to learn the basics about this breed. In this chapter you will receive a wealth of Bichon Frisé information. By the time you finish this chapter you should have a good understanding of what the Bichon Frisé breed is like and you will be on your way to deciding if this is the right pet for you and your family.

1.) What are Bichon Frisé Dogs?

For the most part, Bichon Frisés are a friendly and playful breed, eager to spend time with family. Although these dogs do require a moderate amount of daily exercise, they are pretty good at entertaining themselves in the house as long as they have enough toys to play with. These dogs are very social as well and they love to be in the company of people and other dogs – they also tend to get along well with children.

The Bichon Frisé dog breed is definitely a companion breed. These dogs crave human attention and they tend to bond closely with their owners. Bichon Frisé are loyal and affectionate, eager to please their owners. This breed is also fairly intelligent and quick to learn. This makes tasks like house-training and obedience training relatively easy. As is true for all dogs, however, it is best that you start your dog with training and socialization as early as possible to prevent the development of behavior problems.

As this breed is so people-oriented, it is not recommended that you leave them alone for long periods of time without another dog to keep them company. This breed needs daily physical exercise as well as mental stimulation/interactive play, every-day. Failure to provide this type of stimulation can potentially to lead to behavioral problems relating to frustration and separation anxiety. This is likely to manifest itself with destructive or aggressive behavior. It is therefore not the dog's fault, but the owner's for not providing basic necessities such as daily exercise.

2.) Facts About Bichon Frisé Dogs

The Bichon Frisé is a small, compact breed with a fluffy "powderpuff" white coat. These dogs are sometimes mistaken for small white poodles because of their curly fur and good-natured personalities. This breed is a small-breed dog that typically stands about 9 to 11 inches (22.9 to 27.9 cm) tall and weighs between 7 and 12 pounds (3.2 to 5.4 kg). The Bichon Frisé may be small, but it has a big personality and a lot of energy. These little dogs love to play and they are always happy to see you.

This breed has a double coat which means that it has a soft, dense undercoat and a coarse outer coat. The undercoat is very soft and the outer coat stands away from the body which gives the Bichon Frisé a full bodied look. As these dogs have such long coats they require frequent grooming and clippings. The most popular clip for this breed follows the lines of the dog's body to give him the full bodied, bouffant look that is the breed's signature. The Bichon Frisé is generally white in color with a dark nose and eyes. However, as stated by the AKC, 'a small amount of buff, cream or apricot shading is permitted in competition'.

The Bichon Frisé is often described as a non-shedding breed but this is not exactly true. This breed does shed but its shed fur gets caught up in the undercoat instead of falling off the dog. If you do not brush or groom this breed often enough, the shed fur will form mats and tangles which can increase the dog's risk for skin problems. It is also important to check the dog's ears frequently because they are covered in fur which makes the likelihood for ear infections higher.

The Bichon Frisé is definitely not a low-maintenance dog. In addition to its grooming needs, this breed requires a lot of daily attention. The Bichon Frisé is very friendly and affectionate with family and it generally gets along with everyone it meets. These dogs are very playful and highly intelligent, so it is recommended that you start training and socialization as early as possible. This breed does have a bit of an independent streak at times, so you need to have a firm and consistent hand in training. With positive reinforcement training methods, however, the Bichon typically learns quickly.

The breed is generally very healthy, and responsible breeding practices will reduce the risk for serious health problems. Like all breeds, however, the Bichon Frisé is prone to developing certain conditions. Some of the conditions to which the Bichon Frisé breed is prone include bladder stones, bladder infections, allergies, patellar luxation, vaccination sensitivity, hip dysplasia, and juvenile cataracts. You should take your Bichon Frisé to the vet every 6 months for a routine check-up and to keep your dog up to date on vaccinations.

One of the best qualities of the Bichon Frisé is that they get along very well with children. These dogs love to romp and play, and they are generally very tolerant of a little rough behavior. It is important that you teach your children how to properly handle a dog however, and do not leave your dog unsupervised with young children. They do get along well with other dogs as long as they receive adequate attention from his human companions. This breed is prone to separation anxiety if left alone for too long, so having another dog for company may help to reduce the risk of this problem.

a) Summary of Bichon Frisé Facts

» Origins: descendant from the Barbichon family of dogs originating in the Mediterranean

» Breed Size: Small

» Height: 9 to 11 inches (22.9 to 27.9 cm)

» Weight: 7 to 12 pounds (3.2 to 5.4 kg)can be up to 16 pound.

» Coat Length: medium-length

» Coat Texture: double; soft, dense under coat and harsh outer coat that stands out from the body

» Color: Generally white but cream, buff or apricot shading is sometimes seen.

» Markings: no markings in purebreds

» Eyes and Nose: black

» Temperament: Inquisitive, friendly, playful, energetic, affectionate, good with kids, intelligent

» Training: very intelligent, generally responds well to training; may be independent, firm and consistent hand in training is recommended; start early. Early, regular socialization is needed for confidence building, and to maintain their friendly, happy playful natures. They are sensitive and will not respond positively to any harsh training methods.

» Exercise Needs: moderate; long daily walk recommended; interactive playtime.

» Grooming: regular daily brushing is recommended. 4 to 6 weekly trimming and bathing.

» Clipping: clipping and trimming is necessary to control the coat; most popular clip follows the lines of the body

- Lifespan: average 12 to 15 years
- Health: generally healthy; may be prone to bladder stones, bladder infections, allergies, patellar luxation, vaccination sensitivity, hip dysplasia, and juvenile cataracts
- Breed History: descendant from the Barbichon family of dogs originating in the Mediterranean; admitted into the AKC Non-Sporting Group in 1972
- AKC Group: Non-Sporting Group
- KC(UK) Group: Toy

3) Bichon Frisé Breed History

The exact origins of the Bichon Frisé are largely unknown, but it is thought to share some ancestry with the Barbet. The Barbet is a French water dog related to the Poodle that dates back to the 1700s. The name Bichon Frisé comes from the Middle French "bichon", meaning "small long-haired dog". Some believe that the name is a shortening of the word "barbichon", meaning "small poodle". In any case, the first Bichon-type dog was bred during the 1300s as a result of a cross between the Maltese and a Poodle.

In the early years of the breed, Bichon-type dogs were divided into four different categories: Bichon Havanese, Bichon Maltese, Bichon Bolognaise, and Bichon Tenerife. All of these breeds originated in the Mediterranean region and, due to their friendly demeanors, they were transported around the world by sailors. These dogs became particularly popular in Spain and it is thought that Spanish seamen introduced the breed to the island of Tenerife. The Tenerife also became popular in France during the Renaissance but it's height of popularity occurred during the late 1500s in the court of Henry III.

By the time the 19th century came around, the popularity of the breed had waned and it was largely considered a "common dog," often found running the streets. In 1934 the kennel club of France, the Société Centrale Canine, wrote the first breed standard. The breed once more became popular in conjunction with the success of Herge's book, The Adventures of Tintin, which featured a fluffy white dog. At the time, the breed was known by two names, Bichon and Tenerife. So the president of the Fédération Cynologique Internationale proposed a single name for the breed, Bichon Frisé.

The Bichon Frisé was first introduced in the United States around 1955 and the first U.S.born litter occurred a year later. Around 1959, two U.S. breeders acquired specimens of the breed. These two kennels are credited with the development of the breed in the United States. In 1971, the Bichon Frisé was admitted into the AKC's Miscellaneous class but in 1972 was switched to the Non-Sporting Group. The first Bichon Frisé to win Best in Show at the Westminster Kennel Club Dog Show did so in 2001. The breed is currently ranked among the top 40 breeds in the United States based on registration statistics.

Chapter Two:

What to Know Before You Buy

Now that you know the basics about the Bichon Frisé breed, including some background, you may be ready to learn some specifics about keeping these dogs as pets. Before you decide whether or not the Bichon Frisé is the right pet for you, take the time to learn about licensing your Bichon Frisé, keeping your Bichon Frisé with other pets, the costs associated with these dogs, and some pros and cons for the Bichon Frisé breed. With this information in mind you will be able to make an informed decision.

1.) Do You Need a License

Becoming a pet owner is a big responsibility. When you bring your dog home, he immediately becomes your responsibility. You must therefore do your part to take care of him as best you can. Not only do you need to feed and walk your Bichon Frisé, but you also need to take care of some practical responsibilities including licensing your new pet. Before you buy a Bichon Frisé you should take the time to learn whether a license is required in your area. If so, to take the proper steps to obtain one. In this section you will learn about licensing requirements for Bichon Frisés in the United States and in the United Kingdom.

a.) Licensing Bichon Frisés in the U.S.

There are no federal requirements regarding the licensure of dogs in the United States. Rather, these requirements are made at the state level. Before you buy a Bichon Frisé puppy or an adult Bichon Frisé you need to apprise yourself of local dog licensing requirements. Most states require dog owners to license their dogs and, in order to obtain a license, your dog must also be up-to-date on rabies vaccinations. Obtaining a license for your dog is not difficult. Try asking your veterinarian for information or contact your local council instead.

Even if your state does not mandate that you license your Bichon Frisé dog, it is still a good idea to do it anyway. When you license your dog you will need to provide contact information for yourself. If your dog gets lost and is still carrying his license, whoever finds him will be able to use that information to contact you. Obtaining a dog license requires you to fill out a simple form and to pay a fee around $25 (£16.25). You must renew your license each year, although you may have the option to purchase a five-year license or a lifetime license in some states.

b.) Licensing Bichon Frisés in the U.K.

Licensing requirements for dogs in the U.K. are a little different than they are in the U.S. Dog licensing in the UK was abolished in 1987. However, licensing is still mandatory in Northern Ireland, and you can find further details from the website link at the end of the paragraph. Northern Ireland mandates that all dogs carry a license, and the only exception is for assistance dogs and police dogs. Bichon Frisé puppies may be able to get away without a license until they are 6 months old as long as the owner of the puppies is the owner of the mother as well. Dog licenses are renewable annually, just like U.S. licenses. For further information regarding licenses please consult the following link:

http://www.nidirect.gov.uk/dog-licensing-and-microchipping

Important Update 2016:

Please note that as of 6th April 2016 it is compulsory for any dog owner in England to microchip their dog. At the time of press Scotland and Wales were working towards compulsory micro-chipping by April 2016. To confirm whether this applies to you, please check with your vet.

Failure to comply may result in a fine of £500. What this means is that you as the owner of a non micro-chipped dog, will be served a notice of 21 days to comply. If after 21 days of non compliance, the owner will face a £500 fine.

Please have a look at the following web links for further information.

https://www.petlog.org.uk/breeders/compulsory-microchipping-faqs/

http://www.bva.co.uk/News-campaigns-and-policy/Policy/Companion-animals/Microchipping/

2.) How Many Bichon Frisés Should You Keep?

The Bichon Frisé are very social, friendly dogs that get along well with other dogs. Additionally, the Bichon Frisé are people-oriented and require a lot of attention from their owners. For this reason, it is not recommended that you leave your Bichon Frisé alone for long periods of time. If you do, he may develop separation anxiety, or begin chewing household furnishings or worse still, electrical cables. If you work a full-time job and are away from home for long periods of time, it may be beneficial to get two Bichon Frisé so they can keep each other company in your absence.

A pair of dogs play, interact and bond. A pair of dogs is easier on the conscience because you are not leaving a dog completely alone whilst you are at work or socializing. They have the company of one another, which is a much better option for the dog. Some shelters are looking to re-home dogs in established pairs.

This said, a pair can be difficult to handle if they form a pack like mentality and become reactive on walks and in the home. All dogs have individual personalities so the way that a pair of dogs react will really depend on the nature of each dog. Although Bichon Frisés are generally amiable, friendly dogs, again two dogs can develop the pack mentality and become a hustle of growling and barking excitement on walks. If you are looking at puppies though, taking two from the litter is not usually a good idea if you yourself want to be an integral part of your dog's emotional life.

Puppies that are taken from the same litter will be very bonded with each other and as they reach adolescence one of two things can happen. Firstly they may only focus on each other making them difficult to train and control. Secondly they may begin to compete, causing friction between them. That said, the pair could just as easily settle down and be happy together but it is important that you are aware of the risks. If you want two Bichon Frisé dogs because of all of the positive points of a bonded pair, then you can either look for a pair in rescue or bring one dog home, spend a few months getting to know the dog, socializing him or her perfectly, then look for another dog to join your family. This is an approach that will work well with dogs of all ages. You may find that one Bichon Frisé dog and a dog of a different breed get on really well together instead of a pair of Bichon Frisés. Raising one Bichon Frisé puppy can take a lot of time an energy so you should think carefully before bringing home two of them. If you work a full-time job and are not home a lot during the day, the Bichon Frisé might not be the right breed for you. Having a second dog to keep your Bichon Frisé company might help but it will not be a substitute for the level of human interaction this breed craves.

3.) Do Bichon Frisé Get Along with Other Pets & Children?

For the most part, the Bichon Frisé gets along well with other pets. Your best bet for making sure that your dog gets along with other household pets is to bring the puppy up with those pets. Proper socialization and training from an early age will ensure that your Bichon Frisé dog gets along well with other dogs and household pets.

If raised from puppies, with smaller pets such as cats and rabbits, they tend to bond and become good friends. Keep in mind though that if you bring an adult Bichon Frisé to your home, you'll need to be careful with pets such as rabbits, guinea pigs and cats initially. An adult dog may well chase, attack and potentially kill anything unusual to them. Hopefully your Bichon Frisé will soon get used to other pets as a part of the family. But certainly in the early stages, they should never be left unsupervised with other animals.

They are great with children, and kind with one another. Nonetheless, this could lead them to becoming vulnerable to attacks from other dogs or being mishandled by young children. They are generally not known to growl or snap, and only if relentlessly provoked. It is therefore important that you socialize your Bichon Frisé puppy with children as soon as he comes into your home. Children should be taught to respect and care for the puppy and told to never tease or hurt them. They are not a toy and should never be treated as such. In these early stages, please do supervise children handling and playing with the new puppy. Everything will be strange to the puppy including excitable, energetic children, but they will soon get used to each other and accept each other as part of the family.

4) A Boy or a Girl

A lot of prospective dog owners choose a female as they wish to breed from them at some point. However, if this is something you are considering, please don't be tempted to breed with her on a continuous basis. It is always good to have one litter to keep the generation of your beloved pet going. However a common potential draw back with never breeding from her is the potential for developing pyometra later in life. This is a uterine infection, that requires the removal of the female reproductive system.

When deciding upon a male or female, it sometimes comes down to the preference of the owner or the personality of the dog. Two dogs of the same breed and the same litter can have completely different personalities. But sometimes, dog owners who have always had dogs for years simply prefer either a dog or a bitch.

5.) Ease and Cost of Care

Another important factor you need to consider before bringing home Bichon Frisé puppies, is the cost associated with their care. Owning a dog is a big responsibility and it is up to you to provide for your dog's every need. Not only does this include shelter, but it also includes food, veterinary care, grooming, and exercise. Before you decide to buy a Bichon Frisé dog you should consider the costs associated with keeping a dog and make sure that you can cover them. In this section you will find a list of initial costs and monthly costs associated with Bichon Frisé ownership as well as an overview and explanation of each cost.

A.) INITIAL COSTS

PLEASE NOTE: The following is offered as a guideline only, as costs can vary depending on where you are located, where you buy from, the time you are looking etc.

The initial costs for owning a Bichon Frisé include those costs you must cover to purchase your dog and to prepare your home for his/her arrival. Initial costs include the purchase price, a crate or kennel, spay/neuter surgery, vaccinations, microchipping, and other accessories.

Below is a summary table of each expense, followed by an explanation and breakdown of costs

Purchase Price – The purchase price for Bichon Frisé puppies may vary from one Bichon Frisé breeder to another.

A purebred Bichon puppy sells for an average of about $700 to $1,000 (£455 to £650),although you may find cheaper or more expensive than this. Puppies from champion show dogs could easily be around $2500 (£1625) or more.

A more popular and recognized Bichon Frisé breeder will have more

Initial Costs for Bichon Frisé Dogs

Cost	One Dog	Two Dogs
Purchase Price	$700 to $1,000 (£455 to £650)	$1,400 to $2,000 (£910 to £1,300)
Crate or Kennel	$35 (£22.75)	$70 (£45.50)
Spay/Neuter	$50 to $200 (£32.50 to £130)	$100 to $400 (£65 to £260)
Vaccinations	$50 (£32.50)	$100 (£65)
Micro-chipping	$15 to $50 (£9.75 to £32.50)	$30 to $100 (£19.50 to £65)
Accessories	$100 (£65)	$200 (£130)
Total	$950 to $1,435 (£618 to £933)	$1900 to $2,870 (1,236 to £1,866)

*These rates are based on a conversion rate of $1 U.S. to £0.65 U.K. Rates are subject to change.

expensive puppies, especially if high-quality, and good representatives of the sire and dam are used. You are also likely to find that this type of breeder will not advertise and therefore only come via word of mouth or through organizations such as AKC or KC UK.

Where ever you purchase, always try and ensure that your Bichon Frisé has a written health guarantee against hereditary and congenital defects.

Crate or Kennel – Having a crate or kennel for your Bichon Frisé puppy is very important. Not only will it be instrumental in house-training, but it will give your puppy a place of his own in the house where he can retreat if he wants a nap or just needs a break from people. You will need to upgrade your puppy's crate as he grows, but to start with, a small crate should only cost you about $35 (£22.75) or so.

Spay/Neuter Surgery – Having your Bichon Frisé puppy spayed or neutered is incredibly important, especially if you do not plan to breed your dog. There are a number of opinions as to when is the best time to spay a female dog. Some vets recommend that you spay or neuter your puppy around 6 months of age to reduce the risk for certain types of cancer. The ASPCA points out that the traditional age to spay is 6 to 9 months. The Blue Cross further asserts that there is no benefit in delaying spay surgery until after their first season. They also suggest that certain health benefits are reduced if you wait until after the first season. Others will assert that the dog should be fully mature and developed, consequently carrying out spay surgery in between the first and second season. Always discuss this with your veterinary surgeon. Spay/neuter surgery can be very expensive if you go to a regular veterinarian. But there are plenty of low-cost clinics out there that offer affordable spay/neuter surgery options. If you go to a clinic or shelter, neuter surgery will very likely only cost you $50 to $100 (£32.50 to £65) and spay surgery with a private vet will generally cost $100 to $200 (£65 to £130).

Vaccinations – Before your Bichon Frisé puppy turns one year old, he/she will need to get certain vaccinations. If you buy your puppy from a reputable breeder the pup may already have a few of these vaccinations taken care of by the time you take him home. Speak to your veterinarian about a vaccination schedule for your puppy and plan to spend up to $50 (£32.50) for your puppy's initial vaccinations.

Micro-chipping – Not only may you need to have your puppy licensed, but you should also consider micro-chipping as well. A dog license is worn on a collar around your dog's neck but a microchip is implanted underneath the skin so that it cannot be lost. The procedure does not hurt your dog and it only takes a few minutes to complete. You should be able to have it done at your local animal shelter for as little as $15 (£9.75) at a shelter or up to $50 (£32.50) for a veterinarian to do it.

Other Accessories – In addition to your dog's crate, you will also need certain accessories. These accessories will include a food dish, water dish, collar, leash, grooming tools, and toys. What you spend on each of these items is up to you and the cost will vary depending on quality. You should expect to pay about $100 (£65) for these accessories, though you could easily spend $200 (£130) or more if you purchased high-quality or designer items.

b.) Monthly Costs

Part of being a responsible dog owner is meeting the needs of your dog. If you cannot comfortably cover the initial costs and monthly costs described in this section you should not purchase a Bichon Frisé dog.

The monthly costs for owning a Bichon Frisé include those recurring costs you must cover on a monthly ongoing basis. Monthly costs include the food and treats, veterinary care, grooming, license renewal, and other costs.

On the next page you will find a summary table of each monthly expense.

Below you will find an overview of each expense and an estimate:

Food and Treats –Because the Bichon Frisé is a small-breed dog, your food costs will not be too high. Costs may vary depending what kind of food you buy, but it is not recommended that you shop by price. The quality of the food you give your dog has a direct impact on his health and wellbeing, so do not skimp. You should plan to spend about $30 (£19.50) on a large bag of dog food that will last you about one month. In addition to food, you should budget an extra $10 (£6.50) per month for treats, especially when you are training your dog.

Veterinary Care – In order to keep your Bichon Frisé in good health, you should plan to visit the veterinarian about every 6 months. Your Bichon Frisé puppy may need more frequent visits during the first year for vaccinations, but after that, two visits per year should be adequate. You should expect to spend about $40 (£26) per visit which, with two visits per year, averages to about $7 (£4.55) per month.

Grooming – As the Bichon Frisé is double coated, and has a coat that grows fairly quickly, you will need to take him to a professional groomer to get trimmed/clipped. If you acquire the correct knowledge and instruction, you may be able to do this yourself. Most owners recommend grooming your dog every 4 to 6 weeks which equates to about 8 to 12 visits per year. You should expect to spend about $50 (£32.50) per visit, so the average monthly cost for grooming at most evens out to about $50 (£32.50) per month. Obviously this can get quite expensive, so it may be worth considering doing this yourself.

License Renewal – (Again, this does not apply to every country or even U.S. state)License renewal is not a major expense. You only need to have your dog's license renewed once a year and it generally costs

Monthly Costs for Bichon Frisé Dogs

Cost	One Dog	Two Dogs
Food and Treats	$40 (£26)	$80 (£52)
Veterinary Care	$7 (£4.55)	$14 (£9.10)
Grooming	$50 (£32.50)	$100 (£65)
License Renewal	$2 (£1.30)	$4 (£2.60)
Other Costs	$15 (£9.75)	$30 (£19.50)
Total	$114 (£74)	$228 (£148)

*These rates are based on a conversion rate of $1 U.S. to £0.65 U.K. Rates are subject to change.

about $25 (£16.25) which averages to just $2 (£1.30) per month.

Other Costs – In addition to veterinary care and grooming costs, there are other costs which you may need to cover once in a while. These costs may include new toys, replacement collars as your Bichon Frisé grows, new grooming tools, cleaning products, and more. To be safe, you should budget about $15 (£9.75) per month for these additional costs.

IMPORTANT: Once again, part of being a responsible dog owner is meeting the needs of your dog. If you cannot comfortably cover the initial costs and monthly costs described in this section you should not purchase a Bichon Frisé dog.

6.) Pros and Cons for Bichon Frisé Dogs

Bichon Frisé are excellent companion dogs and they make great pets, but they are not the right choice for everyone. In addition to considering the costs of keeping a Bichon Frisé you should also think about the pros and cons for the breed. You will find a list of pros and cons for Bichon Frisé dogs listed below:

Pros for Bichon Frisé Dogs

- Small-breed dog, well-suited to apartment/flat, condo and urban life

- Very friendly by nature, great family pet
- Good watchdogs that generally barks at strangers. But not a hostile breed, and does usually make friends easily.
- Generally gets along well with children and other dogs
- Very intelligent, responds well to training and learns quickly
- Low(Non)-shedding breed, though it does require regular grooming and brushing; may be a good option for allergy sufferers
- Generally a healthy breed,
- Does not require a lot of food or space

Cons for Bichon Frisé Dogs

- Fairly high-maintenance breed, needs a lot of attention from its owners
- Requires regular professional grooming every four to six weeks, can be expensive. (Unless you have the time and confidence to do it yourself)
- May develop behavior problems or separation anxiety if neglected

Chapter Three:

Purchasing Bichon Frisé Dogs

If, after carefully reviewing the information in the previous chapter, you have decided that a Bichon Frisé is the right dog for you, then you can consider buying one. Buying a Bichon Frisé puppy is not necessarily as simple as stopping in to your local pet store. You need to be very careful about where you buy your puppy to ensure that it will be healthy. In this chapter you will find information about finding Bichon Frisé puppies for sale from Bichon Frisé breeders U.K. and Bichon Frisé breeders in the U.S. You will also find tips for selecting a reputable breeder and a healthy puppy.

THE most important thing to consider when buying any dog not just a Bichon Frisé, is the health of the puppy. The following will give you a lot to think about in terms of choosing a reputable, preferably highly recommended breeder, and consequent health testing etc.

PLEASE NOTE: The following offers as much information as I am aware about pitfalls and potential problems you may encounter with certain breeders. However, I need to add at this point that a Kennel Club certificate does not necessarily guarantee that the dog you have bought is the same as the pedigree suggests. As unbelievable as this may sound, some unscrupulous breeders have been exposed and prosecuted for selling puppies with false KC registered papers. In some cases the puppies have not even been the breed they were supposed to be and at worse, had major health problems or potential physical defects.

Unfortunately in this day and age of scammers and fraudsters, some un-reputable breeders have been known to pass on puppies with falsified papers. You can also do all the checks you like on a breeder that is registered with the KC and has council approval, but your research and investigations should not stop there. The Kennel Club (UK) does have their 'assured breeder scheme', which was set up to protect dog purchases. Effectively they list breeders who have been checked and verified by the Kennel Club. You can search this at the link at the end of the paragraph. When you click on a breed, it gives you the following message, that if there is a green tick beside the breeder that 'This Symbol indicates that a breeder has had a successful inspection carried out to standards assessed by the United Kingdom Accreditation Service (UKAS). These standards were formally introduced in January 2013 and only Kennel Club Assured Breeders that have completed a successful visit since that date are issued with a UKAS Certificate'

http://www.thekennelclub.org.uk/services/public/acbr/Default.aspx

In addition, you may also find the following links useful:

http://pedigreedogsexposed.blogspot.co.uk/2013/12/the-discredited-breeder-scheme-kennel.html

Please do research as much as you can. It is a good idea to visit many Bichon Frisé kennels, and to speak to as many breeders as possible

1) Ethical Bichon Frisé Breeders

Choosing which breeder to deal with, is just as important as deciding which breed to get. Buying from poor sources such as puppy mills and backyard breeders is a bad choice, and contributes to the continuing overpopulation of pets, and even to large numbers of dogs surrendered at shelters today.

A well-respected Bichon Frisé breeder will usually be able to give you a list of references. This list should contain the names of people that have bought puppies from that breeder over the past few years. The Bichon Frisé breeder should also have his veterinarian available to answer any questions you may have about the health history of the puppies, and the breeder's adult dogs. If your Bichon Frisé breeder is reluctant to give you any information related to veterinary care or previous buyers, this should raise a red flag, and you are probably best to look elsewhere!

Ask whether or not a written health guarantee will be made available. In many instances, the Bichon Frisé breeder that provides all this information is a good breeder.

PLEASE NOTE: I am bound to be repeating myself here, but if at all possible, purchase a puppy whereby the parents have been health tested.

The only exception I would ever make to only purchasing a puppy from health tested parents is adopting a rescue dog. I have rescued a number of dogs that I had no idea about their historical pedigree or health test history. These dogs were exceptionally healthy and only ever had minor ailments. Perhaps I was lucky, but in a lot of cases these rescue dogs are desperate for loving forever homes. I would certainly take a rescue dog any day, regardless of possible health issues. However, the choice ultimately has to be yours.

A useful site which lists breeders in the UK who health test parent dogs is as follows:

http://www.champdogs.co.uk/breeds/bichon-frise/breeders

You should find breeders that health test the parent dogs, highlighted in red.

Health tests are not a Kennel Club requirement for the Bichon Frisé, or any other breed. However, many breeders do believe in using the tests available because they have a strong ethical belief in the care and welfare of the breed. If at all possible, deal with these breeders only. If a breeder does not routinely supply a puppy that has been health checked, they may suggest that you can have this done by your own veterinarian.

There are a few other things to consider when buying a Bichon Frisé puppy and if you carry out careful research right at the start then you can be sure that you bring home the right dog for you.

There are many good reasons for choosing a puppy carefully, most of which people are generally unaware. It's easy for us to be trusting of breeders and those that sell puppies. But in actual fact dog breeders need to be chosen extra carefully for the following reasons;

» Puppy genetic background.

» Puppy health.

» Puppy social skills.

» Welfare of the puppy parents

Irresponsible breeding is the main reason for unwanted and sick dogs in the Western world today. When genetic testing is not carried out; the temperament of the parent dogs is not considered. If the puppy is not socialized from as early as birth then as the pup matures to adulthood, the dog may well have problems. If you buy a puppy from an irresponsible breeder, the dog is at risk of health or behavioral problems, or maybe even both, at any time in his life.

The only dog breeder to consider is the one that has a conscience. This is the type that loves the breed and only breeds one or two litters. They will also carry out all of the testing required before making a decision to breed a litter. This type of breeder knows about puppy socialization. They also know about genetic health, and dog welfare is at the forefront of their minds.

The good dog breeder has a list of people wanting the puppies before they even allow the parent dogs to mate. They are extremely interested in finding the correct puppy home, and are not afraid to turn people away. The good breeder does not have to use classified sites, Facebook or newspapers to advertise their puppies. They are not cagey about the parent dogs and they will always, without fail, allow you to see the puppies with their Mother in the home environment.

You may even feel interviewed, on your initial phone call, by a dog breeder if you are looking for a puppy. If this happens then you can be pretty much certain that you are enquiring about much loved and well-bred Bichon Frisé puppies. In addition to asking you a lot of questions the good dog breeder will state that they must always be given the option to take the dog back, at any point during its life, if you can no longer care for it. There may even be a contract.

The puppies will be wormed, health checked, vaccinated and at least eight weeks old before they leave their Mother.

2) Beware of the Puppy Farmer!

The opposite side to the ethical breeder is the 'puppy farmer'. Not everyone with Bichon Frisé puppies for sale is a good and ethical dog breeder. In actual fact some care very little about the dogs in their charge.

This is a trap that most people fall into when looking for a puppy. It's actually hard to believe that people would farm dogs in this way, but it happens and if you are looking for a puppy, you can be sure that at least some of your options are puppy farmed dogs.

The pet store puppy is usually from a puppy mill as are those sold in big sized litters through classifieds. This is not to say that buying puppies from classified ads is a bad thing. Some excellent puppies are available this way, and often this is the most convenient way a reputable 'hobby' breeder can find potential puppy parents. Although all puppies look the same, usually healthy, clean, fluffy and with that addictive puppy scent, the farmed puppy is very different indeed.

The puppy mill is a harrowing place. It is much the same as a factory farm for pigs, cows and chickens. Dogs are kept in small pens and bred from, each time the dog comes into season. The Mother dog is stressed throughout her life and often puppy farmed dogs never go for a walk. They rarely, if at all, receive veterinary attention.

The dogs are kept in small pens and rarely cleaned up after. They are also rarely handled and are fed on cheap food. As you can probably imagine, bacteria thrives in this type of environment and stress levels are high. With the ever increasing link between low quality commercial food and illness, a puppy born and whelped in this type of environment will have a very poor start in life.

Studies are increasingly showing that the presence of stress in a pregnant mother dog can lead to flighty and fearful puppies with the behavior only showing up in the dog's adolescent and adult life. So how do you recognize a puppy farmer or a puppy that has been bred for money alone?

The signs of a puppy farmer are quite easy to spot when you know what to look for. The important thing to remember with this type of dog breeder is that the most important thing to them is money, and the way that they act will betray this.

Warning signs when deciding on a dog breeder are as follows;

» The breeder will have a lot of dogs available and often of different breeds.

» The puppy may be quite cheap.

» There will be no proof of worming, vaccination or veterinary checks.

» Meeting the mother of the puppy will not be possible.

» The breeder will not allow you to see the puppy in the whelping environment.

» The puppy will be younger than eight weeks old when it is sold.

» The breeder will ask very few questions about the home you are offering.

» The breeder will offer to deliver or meet you somewhere with the puppy.

It may be tempting to buy a puppy from this type of breeder anyway and see it as a sort of rescue attempt. This is highly inadvisable because the puppy farmer only exists as a result of people buying their puppies. Therefore to buy a dog in this way is funding the cruel practice of puppy farming. The risk of genetic and environmental health problems caused by bad care of the parent dogs and their offspring from pregnancy onwards, is greatly increased when buying any puppy from a puppy farmer.

3.) Where to Buy Bichon Frisé Dogs

If you have decided that the Bichon Frisé is the right breed for you, your next step is to find a Bichon Frisé for sale. Finding a Bichon Frisé puppy may not be as simple as just stopping in to your local pet store. Even if it were that easy, buying a puppy from a pet store may not be your best option. In this section you will find tips for buying a Bichon Frisé in the U.S. and in the U.K. You will also find information about Bichon Frisé rescue dogs.

Apologies if you are based elsewhere. But please be aware that you simply need to make contact with similar organizations listed here for your location. Additionally, Google searched for [Health Tested Bichon Frisés for sale, [your area/country]], will doubtless provide appropriate results.

a.) Buying in the U.S.

When it comes to buying puppies in the United States you have two main options; a pet store or an independent breeder. As mentioned previously, unfortunately, many pet stores receive their stock from puppy mills. Again, a puppy mill is a breeding facility where dogs are kept in squalid conditions and forced to breed until they are no longer able; they are then disposed of. The puppies that come from puppy mills may be inbred or bred from unhealthy stock which means that they too are likely to be unhealthy. Buying from a pet store is generally not a good option unless you know exactly where the puppy came from and you can confirm that it is from a reputable breeder.

When you buy a puppy from a reputable breeder you are assured that the breeding stock is in good health. Most reputable breeders put their breeding stock through genetic testing before breeding to ensure that they are not going to pass on congenital conditions such as hip dysplasia or progressive retinal atrophy. Responsible breeders also know a lot about the breed and can help you to decide whether it is a good choice for you.

In the next section you will find more detailed information about choosing a reputable breeder. For now, however, you will find a list of U.S. Bichon Frisé breeders next, which may have Bichon Frisé puppies for sale:

The following are breeders which at the time of press, where actively health testing the parent dogs.

PLEASE NOTE: The following, to the best of my knowledge are all good, reputable breeders. However, I am in no way connected/affiliated to them, nor am I endorsing/recommending anyone in particular. I urge you as always to do a thorough research of all possibilities, consider all options and make your own mind up.

American Kennel Club (AKC)

http://marketplace.akc.org/puppies/bichon-frise

Gemstone Bichon Frisés

http://www.gemstonebichons.com/puppies.html

Whitebred Bichon Frisés

http://www.whitebredbichons.com/

Astartes Bichons

http://www.astartefrenchiesand-bichons.com/About-Us.html

Victoire's Bichons

http://www.victoirebichons.com/about_victoire

MusicBox Bichons Showboat Bichons

http://www.musicboxbichons.com/about-us/

Showboat Bichons

http://www.showboatbichons.com/

The American Kennel Club has a useful link to breeders and available Bichon Frisé puppies as follows:

https://www.apps.akc.org/apps/classified/search/landing_breed.cfm

You can also find Bichon Frisé breeders using the Breeders Club directory:

http://breedersclub.net/

B.) BUYING IN THE U.K.

Purchasing Bichon Frisé puppies in the U.K. is very similar to buying them in the U.S. Always do your research before buying Bichon Frisé puppies in the U.K. to ensure that the Bichon Frisé puppies for sale have been bred properly. The last thing you want is to pay for a puppy from a breeder just to find that it is unhealthy. On the next page you will find a list of breeders with Bichon Frisé puppies for sale in the U.K.

AGAIN PLEASE NOTE: The following, to the best of my knowledge are all good, reputable breeders. However, I am in no way connected/affiliated to them, nor am I endorsing/recommending anyone in particular. I urge you as always to do a thorough research of all possibilities, consider all options and make your own mind up.

Fribonch Bichon Frise uk

http://www.fribonch.co.uk/

Kennel Club: Find a breeder

http://www.thekennelclub.org.uk/services/public/findapuppy/Default.aspx?id=Bichon+Frise

Bobander Bichon Frisé

http://www.bobanderbichons.co.uk/

Magstarai Bichons

http://www.magstaraibichons.co.uk/

Kennel Club Assured Breeders (KCAB)

http://www.thekennelclub.org.uk/services/public/acbr/Default.aspx?breed=Bichon+Frise

There are others that you could locate by doing a Google search along the lines of [Bichon Frisé Puppies For Sale Uk]. Again my emphasis is always 'Health Tested'.

However, that is not to say that a certain breeder you may find, does not have excellent healthy puppies for sale.

You can also research sites such as

http://www.pets4homes.co.uk/.

This is probably what you might term a classified site. I have seen reputable breeders with adverts on this site. But please do not assume that all breeders advertising on here will not be 'puppy farm' agents also. Again, please bear in mind the advice given in this book. Above all, do your research and do not rush into anything without thoroughly checking things out first.

c. Adopting a Rescue Dog

Unless you specifically have your heart set on a Bichon Frisé puppy, you may be able to find an adult Bichon Frisé at a local animal shelter or Bichon Frisé rescue. There are many benefits to adopting an adult dog versus buying a puppy. For one thing, adoption prices are much lower than the cost of purchasing a puppy from a breeder. Adoption rates typically range from $100 to $200 (£65 to £130). Furthermore, when you adopt an adult dog it may already be house-trained and have some obedience training.

While raising a puppy is great, it can take a lot of time and commitment and it can be a challenge. If you do not want to deal with a puppy having accidents in your house or if you want to avoid the whole teething stage, adopting an adult dog may be the right choice. Furthermore, when you buy a puppy from a Bichon Frisé breeder you do not know what its temperament and personality will be when it grows up. If you adopt an adult dog, what you see is what you get.

If you are thinking of adopting a Bichon Frisé rescue dog, consider one of the following rescues or shelters:

U.S.A Bichon Frisé Rescue Centers

Animal League

http://www.animalleague.org/adopt-a-pet/dogs/purebreed-rescue-adoption/bichon-frise.html?referrer=https://www.google.co.uk/

Adopt-a-Pet

http://www.adoptapet.com/s/adopt-a-bichon-frise

Bichon FurKids

http://www.bichonfurkids.org/

Bichon Rescue Brigade

http://www.bichonrescuebrigade.org/

Bichon Frise Club of America Charitable trust

http://bichonrescue.org/

Bichon Rescue Tennessee

http://bichonfriseusa.com/brtn/pix.htm

Small Paws Rescue

http://www.smallpawsrescue.org/

UK Bichon Frisé Rescue Centers

Bichon Frisé Rescue

http://www.bichonfriserescue.co.uk/

Kennel Club: Bichon Frise Breed Rescue

http://www.thekennelclub.org.uk/services/public/findarescue/Default.aspx?breed=6148

Many Tears Animal Rescue

http://www.manytearsrescue.org/dogslookingforhomes.php

Battersea

http://www.battersea.org.uk/apex/weblanding?pageId=007-dogslanding&t=dog

Oldies Club

http://www.oldies.org.uk/

In addition to the above, please check your local RSPCA / ASPCA and any local dog rescue centres, by doing a Google search such as the following: 'Rescue dogs [home town]

4) Fostering

Fostering is an excellent option if you are unsure about whether you can commit to looking after a dog on a permanent basis.

The purpose of fostering dogs and other animals is to prevent euthanasia. Fostering can also provide better alternatives for all animals, by providing a safe and nurturing temporary home. Fostering also increases the live-release rate of all pets, and reduces the number of dogs and cats that die from homelessness. Many rescue groups rely on foster homes to do their great work. These rescue groups will also at times end up paying for dogs to board at kennels when they do not have enough foster homes to turn to.

Fostering entails a temporary arrangement of a limited time where a person takes care of a dog, until a permanent home can be found for that dog. It is not adopting. However, quite often, many foster parents will end up adopting the dog that they foster.

a) Bichon Frisé Fostering

This is an arrangement between a shelter or a Bichon Frisé rescue group and the person agreeing to foster. In this case there will be a contract between you and the Bichon Frisé rescue group, detailing the responsibilities between both parties such as whom is responsible for veterinary bills, training, transport and food.

b) Questions To Ask Before Fostering a Bichon Frisé

It is very likely that the rescue center organizing the fostering would answer the following questions and more anyway. But it is good for you to be aware of the type of issues you will face, such as the examples below.

» How long will I be fostering this Bichon Frisé?

» What happens should I change my mind, or if I'm

not a good fit?

- What should I do if my foster Bichon Frisé does not get along with my other pets?
- What should I do if there's a veterinary emergency?
- Who pays the veterinary bills? Would that include all veterinary treatments?
- Is my foster Bichon Frisé currently on any medication, or in need of ongoing treatment?
- Do I speak with potential adopters, screening them and possibly introducing my Bichon Frisé to them?
- Will I be required to bring my foster Bichon Frisé to certain adoption events and if so, how many times a month?
- Does the Bichon Frisé have any behavioral issues that require training, and can you provide this? Can I choose my own trainer?
- Who pays for dog food, veterinary supplies and dog training supplies? This is likely to be you but is worth asking as some may be available via the center.
- If my foster Bichon Frisé has any behavioral problems, whom can I contact?
- Do I get to keep him permanently?

5.) Choosing a Reputable Breeder

PLEASE REMEMBER:

You should not necessarily buy the first Bichon Frisé puppy for sale that you come across. You need to do your research and make sure that you are purchasing from a responsible breeder. A responsible Bichon Frisé breeder will be careful about selecting healthy breeding stock and they will keep detailed records of their breeding practices. If the breeder does not appear to be experienced with the Bichon Frisé breed, or with breeding dogs in general, you should look elsewhere.

As well as researching the websites listed earlier, try asking around at your local animal shelter or a veterinarian's office for recommendations. Once you have compiled a list of several breeders you can then go through the list to determine which one is the best option.

Follow the steps below to choose a reputable breeder:

- Visit the website for each breeder, if they have one, and look for important information such as photos of the facilities, the breeder's experience.

- Contact each breeder by phone and ask them questions about their experience with breeding and with Bichon Frisés. If the breeder is hesitant to answer your questions, or if they do not seem knowledgeable and experienced, move on to the next option

- Evaluate the breeder's interest in learning more about you. A reputable breeder will not just sell his puppies to anyone, they should be eager to ask you questions to see if you are a good fit for one of their puppies.

- Narrow your list down to two or three breeders that seem to be a good fit and visit the facilities before you make a commitment to buy a puppy.

- Ask for a tour of the facilities and look to make sure that the dogs are kept in clean conditions and that they appear to be in good health.

- Make sure you see the breeding stock for the puppies that are available to make sure that they are in good health and good specimens of the Bichon Frisé breed.

- Ask to see the puppies that are available and make sure that they are kept in clean conditions. Remember, if they are under 6 weeks of age, the puppies should be kept with the mother until at least 8 weeks old.

- Choose the breeder that you feel is most knowledgeable and experienced, and no just the one that has puppies available. You will also probably get a gut feeling as to whether they are a reputable breeder or not.

- Ask about the process for reserving a puppy. You will probably have to leave a deposit by way of a down payment. In addition, ask what the price includes (vaccinations, worming etc).

- A reputable breeder will offer some kind of health guarantee on the puppy as well as information about the parents to certify its breeding.

6.) Selecting a Healthy Bichon Frisé Puppy

After you have gone through the process of selecting a reputable breeder, your next step is to choose a healthy puppy. While it may be tempting to buy the first puppy that comes up to you with a wagging tail, you need to be a little more cautious about the process. Taking the time to ensure that the puppy is in good health could save you a lot of veterinary bills (not to mention heartache) in the future.

Follow the steps below to pick a healthy puppy:

- » Ask to see all of the puppies at once and spend a few minutes watching how they interact with each other before you approach them.
- » Healthy puppies should be playful and energetic. They should not be lolling around or acting lethargic.
- » Make yourself available to the puppies but do not immediately try to interact. Wait and see which ones are curious enough to approach you.
- » Bichon Frisé puppies are very sociable and playful, so they should be eager to interact with you.
- » Spend a few minutes engaging with each puppy. Play with a toy to gauge the puppy's activity and try petting him to make sure he doesn't respond with fear or aggression.
- » If you can, watch the puppies being fed as well to make sure that they have a healthy appetite. A puppy that does not eat is likely to be sick.
- » Examine the puppies more closely for signs of good health. Do not just look for obvious signs of illness.

Below is a list of what you should look for in different categories:

- » Eyes: bright and clear; no discharge or crust
- » Breathing: quiet and steady; no snorting, coughing, or sneezing
- » Energy: alert and energetic; eager to play
- » Body: The puppy should look well-fed, not too skinny

» Coat: the coat should be clean and healthy without bare patches, flaking skin, or other problems; the color should be uniform

» Hearing: the puppy should react if you clap your hands behind his head

» Vision: the puppy should be able to see clearly if you toss a toy or roll a ball across his line of sight

» Gait: the puppy should move easily without limping or evidence of soreness/stiffness

» Genitals: the genitals should be clean

If the puppies appear to be physically healthy and do not show any behavioral warning signs like aggression, excessive fear, or lethargy, then they are probably a good buy. Once you've assessed the condition of the puppies you can spend some more time playing with them to find out which puppy is a good personality match for you. Keep in mind that the personality and temperament of your puppy might change a little as he grows, but you have some control over that depending on how you train and socialize him over the coming weeks.

7) Naming your puppy

If you have finally chosen the dog or puppy you want then perhaps now is as good a time as any to decide on his name. If you have hopefully bought from a reputable breeder, and are leaving a deposit to then collect him in a few weeks time, then you can get the breeder to start calling him by that name. Never use his name for anything negative or your dog will try his hardest not to respond when he hears it. Always make it positive and fun and soon your dog will know exactly who he is. You probably already have ideas yourself, but if not, please make the name short and sweet. Something like, Daisy, Tess, Max or a name that relates to his appearance such as Patch.

8.) Puppy–Proofing Your Home

Depending on when you visit the breeder, the puppies may not be ready to take home just yet. Again, a responsible breeder will not sell a puppy under 8 weeks old or until the puppies are fully weaned. Even if the puppies are available when you visit you should wait until you have prepared your home before buying the puppy. Below you will find some important steps to take in puppy-proofing your home:

Your Bichon Frisé will want to explore every nook and cranny of his new home. Part of that process involves his teeth. Keep all items that are valuable or dangerous away from him. This particularly includes electrical cables that may be live and therefore the puppy is risking an electric shock and at worse a fatality. Replace them with non-toxic chew-able puppy toys in bright colors. Any chewed items are your responsibility, and you should be aware of this when the puppy sees an interesting thing to chew. They do not see the value or the danger, so please be aware that it is not your Bichon Frisé's fault if something gets chewed. Never use harsh corrections. Not even a tap on the nose. Instead use a firm "No" and replace the item with a chew-able dog toy for teething pups.

Anywhere within your home that your Bichon Frisé puppy is allowed to wander needs to be puppy proofed. This is similar to baby proofing your home, and requires you to go down on hands and knees and see what dangers lurk at puppy eye level.

Puppies enjoy chewing the solid rubberized covering of electrical cords and outlets . Remember, these can result in a fatality. Pups can also pull down electrical appliances by yanking on the cords.

» Prevent your Bichon Frisé from jumping up on any unstable objects like bookcases

» Do not allow your Bichon Frisé access to high decks or ledges, balconies, open windows, or staircases. Instead use baby gates, baby plastic fencing and therefore prevent accidents from happening.

» Keep your doors securely shut and again prevent a potential accident.

» Never slam doors with a Bichon Frisé puppy in the house. Use doorstops to make sure that the wind does not slam a door in your Bichon Frisé's face.

» Clear glass doors also pose a danger since your Bichon Frisé may not see them and run right into one. Use a screen door. Your Bichon Frisé puppy could run right into something at break neck speed.

» Check for toxic plants, medicines, sharp objects, and even dead branches.

The whole point of the preceding is to get you to think about any potential hazards for your Bichon Frisé. Remember, they are relying on you as their guardian, in much the same way as a child.

a) Toxins To Be Aware of in Your Home

» Insecticides

» Human medications

» Household cleaning products

» Foods that we consume that have a toxic effect on dogs such as grapes and chocolates

» Rodenticides

» Plants

» Garden and pool products

» Glass, razors, bathroom products

» Coins, small batteries and other small objects that may easily be ingested

You'll need to watch your Bichon Frisé puppy very carefully for the first few months to make sure that he does not get into harm's way. Usually the kitchen is made into the puppy's room. In this instance, it's best to make sure that all cleaning supplies are removed and placed elsewhere. Bichon Frisé pups are curious, and it can take as little as a few minutes for your puppy to get into a poisonous cleaning product.

b) Checking For Toxins in Puppy Toys

Before purchasing toys for your Bichon Frisé to play with, you'll need to check that they are lead free and cadmium free.

Dog toys that contain DEHP- bis (2-ethylhexl) phthalate have been found to have a huge effect on the reproductive system of rats, even at very low doses. Toy products for example, from Cordura contain no detectable amounts of lead, cadmium, or phthalates. Use non-toxic tennis balls from Planet Dog or other reputable sources.

Non-toxic play toys are very important for all Bichon Frisé puppies that experience stress when left alone. These toys serve as anxiety busters, and give your Bichon Frisé puppy something to do when left alone.

Puppy-hood does not last for very long, and is a very special time in everyone's lives. It is during the Puppy-hood stage that training, playing, socializing and all the preparation that you do with your Bichon Frisé puppy needs to be taken seriously.

c.) Summary for Puppy-Proofing Your Home

» Keep all of your cleaning products and dangerous chemicals stored securely in a cabinet where your puppy will not be able to access it.

» Store all food in the refrigerator or pantry where your puppy can't get it. Any food that you leave out needs to be in a tight-lidded container.

» Make sure that all of your medications and toiletries are stored in drawers or in your medicine cabinet.

» If you own a cat, make sure the litter box is stored somewhere your puppy can't get at it.

» Keep all doors closed to areas of the house that might be dangerous for your puppy (such as the garage or laundry room). You may even want to use baby gates to confine your puppy to whatever room you are in.

- If your yard does not already have a fence, consider having one installed so that your puppy can play outside safely.

- Try not to use tobacco products in the house where your puppy might breathe the smoke. You should also dispose of ash and cigarette butts properly so your puppy doesn't get into them.

- Keep all bodies of water (including sinks, bathtubs, toilets, etc.) covered. Even a small amount of water could pose a drowning risk for a small puppy.

- Keep a lid on all of your trash-cans and, if possible, keep them in a cabinet for an added level of security. You don't want your puppy to chew on something that he could choke on or that may be poisonous to him.

- Keep all electrical cords and loose blinds tied up so your puppy doesn't chew on or trip on the strings. Cover your outlets with outlet covers.

- Check to make sure that none of the plants in your house or on your property are toxic to dogs. If they are, make sure they are well out of your puppy's reach or put a fence around them.

- Make sure you don't leave any small objects on the floor for your puppy to find. This includes things like childrens toys, small articles of clothing, jewelry, and more.

In addition to following these steps to puppy-proof your home you also need to carefully supervise your puppy when he is not in his crate. Your puppy doesn't know what is dangerous, so it is your job to keep him safe.

9) Where Will your Puppy Sleep

Deciding where your puppy will sleep is important. Many people choose to allow a little dog on their bed, which is fine. However, it's important to understand separation anxiety if you sleep with your dog, and are allowing him to be with you at all times. Separation anxiety is caused by over-attachment, and sleeping in your bed can be part of the reason for that.

On the first night when you bring your puppy home, I suggest that you don't leave him alone. Imagine how he would feel after being in the warmth of his nesting area with his mother and siblings to be then completely alone. So make a conscious decision to stay in the room where your puppy will be sleeping for a couple of nights. You can also invest in a very specific puppy comforter meant for the first few nights in a new home, they can be warmed in the microwave and some even have heartbeats.

If your puppy is going to be eventually sleeping alone, then it's not a good idea to allow him to sleep on you. It would be much better to lie on the couch and have him on the ground beside you. That way you can offer a comforting hand when needed but he will be learning to leave behind the warmth of bodies at bedtime. You can introduce the crate right at the beginning if you prefer, or wait until that first couple of nights are over. Eventually you will be able to leave a happily secure puppy in his sleeping place with ease.

An older dog that will be sleeping in another room in the beginning will probably howl and bark for the first few nights. Do not panic though because this is often due to unsettled feelings rather than severe separation anxiety. It usually wears off when the dog begins to feel secure.

10) Setting Up Your Bichon Frisé's Crate

The important thing about introducing your dog, whatever his age, to the crate is to make it a nice place that he finds welcoming. Put a cozy bed, toys and maybe even a stuffed

Kong or other activity toy in the crate and allow your dog to sit in there with the door open to begin with.

If you need to have the crate close to you, in order to make your puppy feel secure, then this is fine too. But remember to then move it away later. The idea is to show your puppy that his crate is a most comfortable bedroom to the point that he chooses it as his resting place, all on his own.

When you do start to close the door, only do it for a short time. The idea is that your dog never thinks that he is going to be trapped against his will. Never just push the dog in and close the door as this can easily cause a phobia.

To make your Bichon Frisé feel at home, place his crate somewhere permanent and place his food and water dishes nearby. You should also place a box with his toys in the area as well. Ideally, your Bichon Frisé's crate should be kept in a location that is not in the middle of household activity but that is not too isolated either. You will be keeping your Bichon Frisé in the crate overnight and when you are away from home during the house-training period, so place the crate somewhere that will not be in the way. If you do not like the idea of confining your

Bichon Frisé to the crate while you are away, you should set up a puppy play yard around the crate so your Bichon Frisé has a little more space. He will still be confined but will be safe from potential hazards. He will be able to move around a little more to play with his toys.

11) Bringing your puppy/adult dog home

When you pick your puppy up from the breeder they are bound to provide some sort of puppy pack. This should include at the very least all of the relevant paper work, including the pedigree and perhaps your new Kennel Club documents. You will also probably receive a health certificate. Always remember to ensure you also receive the following:

1. A diet sheet giving you precise details of when the puppy has been getting his meals, along with the particular food. (Please continue to feed according to this plan, as any sudden changes will affect his digestive system with a possible upset stomach and diarrhea). Do not worry too much if your puppy does not seem to be eating the recommended amount as he may have lost some of his appetite with the upheaval of leaving his mother and siblings.
2. Once he has settled in after a few days he should start to finish his meals. If he is finishing his meals every time then by all means give him more, and again if he leaves some, then cut back slightly.
3. Please also remember that each breeder will have different ideas about how they feed their puppy. Again, do not worry if it is different to what you may have read or been told. The important thing is that he is fed a high quality nutritious diet.
4. We will talk more about feed and feeding next, but just to give you a rough idea of a typical feeding schedule, it may include 4 or 5 separate meals spread out over the day from 7 or 8am to 10 or 11pm. The food the puppy may have been fed could well consist of a quality commercial diet consisting of tinned puppy food with puppy mixer. It could also include cooked fish, scrambled egg, milk and rusk, cooked chicken, vegetables, rice, puppy milk, minced beef/lamb/pork etc. In this day and age of BARF diets, do not be too alarmed to find your puppy has just started a predominantly raw diet of some sort. Whatever the diet, stick to it and if you have a particular diet you would prefer to give him, give this gradually while substituting odd meals until the diet has been changed to your preferred one.

5. Remember to check his worming schedule, that is, when he was last wormed, when he is next due and which worming medication was used.

The First Day Home

If at all possible do not bring home a Bichon Frisé puppy during the holidays when your home is likely to be busy with guests and unusual noises.

Plan to take a few days off from work when you bring your Bichon Frisé puppy home. The next few days will be time consuming, and will need direct supervision from you. This will involve using management tools such as baby gates, crates, exercise pens and puppy pads.

Bringing a new dog home is an exciting and sometimes even a terribly scary time. If you follow the right stages of introduction for the dog though, both into your home and your family, everything should go smoothly.

During this area of the book I will talk about the first few days of a new dog being in your home. I will explain how he may be feeling, how you can communicate properly with your new dog and how to make life easy for all of you within this crucial settling in period. One of the most tempting things to do when you bring a new dog home is celebrate their arrival. Everyone comes to meet the new family member and everyone wants a touch, particularly if the new arrival is a gorgeous Bichon Frisé puppy.

When you bring a new puppy home it is important to remember that he will be confused and learning all of the time. That said, if the young dog has a lot of positive, gentle interaction even from day one, it will be good for him and build his confidence. For this reason the new and young puppy may benefit from some careful visitors. A new adult Bichon Frisé is a different matter. An older dog will need a quiet time in the home for the first few days. The adult dog will not welcome a stream of visitors on day one. The new dog will likely be scared and nervous. Remember that he will have little understanding about what is happening in his life and the best way you can approach this is keep quiet and allow him to get used to the new environment in his own time.

Similarly the dog should be left well alone by family members whilst he is settling in. He can get some positive attention and fuss if he asks for it, but should certainly not be cornered or forced to accept attention. Many canine rescuers have to take dogs back into their care because a problem has occurred on day one or two that could easily have been avoided if the dog was given space and respect to settle into the new home before excited new owners forced their attentions on him.

A dog learns how to react to things, in his life, based upon past experiences. In addition, canine communication is very different to the communication that occurs between people. In actual fact the average new dog owner trying to make friends with a scared Bichon

Frisé by trying to touch him is having the exact opposite effect on their recently arrived dog.

I always ignore a new dog into the home. I barely look at them but offer attention if they ask for it. A very scared dog is allowed to hide where he is happy until he is ready to come out and learn to join in with everyday life in his own time.

There is something that very few people tell you when they present you with a new dog, whatever age he may be. You may think that you have made a mistake. This is an absolutely normal reaction to such a big change in your life. Whether you have brought home a scared teenage dog, a confident adult Bichon Frisé or a needy puppy, you may panic before things settle down. With a puppy, you will worry about why he is crying, whether you are feeding him properly, and how you can be sure that he stays happy and healthy. When you bring home an adult dog, he may show separation anxiety, he may bark in the night for a few days and either be very clingy or completely aloof. An adult dog may be so worried that he shows his teeth in the beginning. It's important not to crowd a new dog and everything will settle down quickly. The dog that is left to settle on his own will have no reason to feel threatened.

So all I can say to you is expect accidents, expect upheaval and expect things to change for a short time; then if the dog settles perfectly, far better than you expected, at least you were prepared

12) First introductions

If you are bringing home a young puppy this will be easier because the puppy, when carefully handled, will generally be accepting of anyone and everyone. In the case of bringing a puppy home, the other animals in the family must be considered. Some older dogs that you may already have, are completely overwhelmed by the new squeaking, face licking, and over keen puppy.

In the beginning they may want to be nowhere near the baby dog. If you live with an older dog, ensure that a puppy does not get walked on and harassed in those early days, particularly if he is worried. Similarly take extra care with the cat and any other pets you may have.

If you are bringing home an older dog, to a home with an existing dog, it is important to take all resources away that may cause friction. So pick up toys, treats and anything that either dog may guard. In particular, I have witnessed more dog fights than anything, where food is concerned. Remember that a new dog may feel insecure, therefore guard things for that reason alone.

It's a good idea to let two older dogs meet on neutral ground. At the park or somewhere similar, rather than just bring the new dog directly home. Walking them together first will allow them to get used to the scent of each other and do the 'meet and greet' without the tension of perceived territory.

13.) Introducing Your Puppy to Children

Bichon Frisés are a very social and people-oriented breed and as previously mentioned, they tend to get along well with children. This doesn't mean, however, that you can just put your puppy in a room with your kids and expect everything to be fine. Just as you need to ensure that your puppy is safe in your home, you also need to teach your children how to properly handle the puppy for their own safety.

Introducing your children to the new dog is important. The kids must learn that the dog is not a toy and a young puppy is very fragile. Never leave your children alone with a new Bichon Frisé of any age as this could be risky for all of them. Carefully explain to your children as much information as you can from this book and you will find that the dog and children become friends for life.

Just as you do between two dogs, watch out for resource guarding between dogs and children. Kids tend to grab at toys and food bowls, particularly the little ones. A dog could easily see this behavior as a threat and snap in return. Similarly remember that any dog will not appreciate uncomfortable poking and prodding before he tells the child to go away, in the only way that he can.

Do not allow your child to follow a dog that has tried to move away from the attentions. This is a recipe for disaster because the dog can feel cornered and think he has to resort to aggression simply to be left alone. If you manage your family well and teach an all-round respect, you will be able to integrate the new dog in perfectly. Before you know it, everyone will be great friends.

Follow the tips below to safely introduce your puppy to children:

Before you bring the puppy home, explain to your children how to properly handle the puppy. Tell them that the puppy is fragile and should be handled with care.

Tell your children to avoid overstimulating the puppy. They need to be calm and quiet when handling him so he does not become frightened.

When it is time to make introductions, have your children sit on the floor in your home and bring the puppy to them.

Place the puppy on the floor near your children and let the puppy wander up to them when he is ready. Do not let your children grab the puppy.

Allow your children to calmly pet the puppy on his head and back when he approaches them. You may even give them a few small treats to offer the puppy.

Let your children pick up the puppy if they are old enough to handle him properly. If the puppy becomes fearful, have them put him carefully back down.

If at any point during your introductions the puppy becomes afraid, you should take him out of the situation and place him in his crate where he can feel safe. Do not let your children scream or act too excited around the puppy until he gets used to them. It will take time for both your children and your puppy to get used to each other and you should supervise all interactions.

Please do remember, that where children are concerned or you already have a few pets, be extra careful of where your attentions go. After all, you want all of your pets to get along with each other, as well as your children. So do not create jealousy by fussing over your new Bichon Frisé puppy and ignoring your other pets. Share your attention equally between all your pets, so that the relationship starts off well. Much of the future relationship between all of your pets, will depend on what happens during the first few days.

With children in the picture, it's important that this new relationship starts off well and gently. If your Bichon Frisé puppy is your first puppy, as stated above, it's best to prepare young children with a firm explanation that all puppies need plenty of rest, quiet and gentleness. Prepare them ahead of time by showing them how to touch a small puppy, and what tone of voice to use i.e. low and comforting.

Children should never scream or run around a small, vulnerable puppy. They also should not pull his ears, tail or any other part of the puppy. It's best to be very firm with your children about all the puppy rules ahead of time.

Chapter Four:

Caring for Bichon Frisé Dogs

Caring for your Bichon Frisé dog requires more than just feeding and walking him – you also need to provide him with a safe place to live. Because Bichon Frisés are such a small breed they are well-suited to apartment, flat or condo life, but that doesn't mean that they do not need space of their own. In this chapter you will learn the basics about making a home for your Bichon Frisé including tips for setting up his crate and other habitat requirements.

In this chapter you will learn the basics about habitat requirements and generally caring for and providing the nutritional needs of your Bichon Frisé. Please be aware that the sections on feeding and nutrition are broad ranging and go into quite a bit of detail. Please do not be tempted to skim read or skip this part. Of all the chapters covered I would say that this is on a level with only buying health tested puppies. It is also probably the most important and sadly over looked aspect of caring for your dog.

1.) Habitat Requirements for Bichon Frisés

As you have already learned, the Bichon Frisé breed remains fairly small so they do not necessarily need a lot of space. This breed is particularly well suited to apartment, flat or condo life, though they will do just as well in a large home. What many potential Bichon Frisé owners want to know, however, is if this breed can be kept outside.

The Bichon Frisé, has a double coat which may help to keep it warm in cold weather. But whilst Bichon Frisé have no trouble enduring cold weather for short periods of time, such as on a walk, they should not be kept primarily as outdoor dogs. In general, the Bichon Frisé should not be kept in extreme temperatures (hot or cold) for long periods of time.

Though Bichon Frisés can do well in a small home environment, they do enjoy having some outdoor space to run and play. If possible, provide your Bichon Frisé with a fenced-in yard where he can play off-leash. If you intend to leave your Bichon Frisé outdoors for more than an hour at a time, consider providing him with a dog house as shelter from heat, cold, and weather. You should also be sure that your dog has plenty of fresh water when he is outside.

2.) Necessary Supplies and Equipment

Bichon Frisés do not need many accessories, but there are a few necessities you will want to have on hand. Some of the necessary supplies and equipment for keeping Bichon Frisés include the following:

» Food and water bowls

» Collar and leash

» Crate or kennel

» Blanket or dog bed

» Grooming supplies

» Assortment of toys

Food and Water Bowls – Your Bichon Frisé's food and water bowls do not necessarily need to be fancy, they just need to be sturdy and sanitary. The best material for food and water dishes is stainless steel because it is easy to clean and does not harbor bacteria. If you prefer, ceramic dishes are a good alternative and they come in a variety of colors to suit your preferences.

Collar and Leash – Having a high-quality collar and leash for your Bichon Frisé is very important. It is also important that these items match your Bichon Frisé's size. When your Bichon Frisé is a puppy you will need a small puppy collar that you can adjust as your puppy grows. Once your dog reaches his adult size you can get a slightly larger collar. The size of your dog's leash may change as he grows as well. When your puppy is young you will want a short leash to use for training and walks. Once your Bichon Frisé grows up and gets some training you can upgrade to a longer leash.

Crate or Kennel – One of the most important accessories you need for your Bichon Frisé is a crate or kennel. If you use it correctly your dog will not view time spent in the crate as punishment and there is no reason to believe that keeping your dog in a crate for short periods of time is cruel. If you use the crate properly whilst training your Bichon Frisé, he will come to view it as a place to call his own. A place where he can go to take a nap or to get some time to himself if he wants it.

When selecting a crate for your Bichon Frisé, size is very important. For the purpose of house training, you want to make sure that the crate is not too big. It should be just large enough for your puppy to stand, sit, lie down, and turn around comfortably. The key to crate training is to get your dog to think of the crate as his home, or his den. Dogs have a natural aversion to soiling their dens. If your puppy's crate is only large enough for him to sleep in, it will be more effective as a house-training tool. When your puppy grows up you can upgrade to a larger crate.

Blanket or Dog Bed – To make your dog's crate more comfortable you should line it with a soft blanket or a plush dog bed. When you are house-training your Bichon Frisé puppy it is best to use an old blanket or a towel, just in case your puppy has an accident. Once your puppy is fully trained however, you can upgrade to a plush dog bed or a thicker blanket that will be more comfortable.

Grooming Supplies – Once again, because the Bichon Frisé's coat grows quickly and because it is fairly thick, it is recommended that you have your dog professionally groomed every 4 to 6 weeks or do it yourself as previously mentioned. However, you still need to brush and comb your dog at home. This will help prevent matting and to keep his coat and skin healthy. The grooming tools you may need for your Bichon Frisé include:

» A small pin brush and/or bristle brush

» Slicker brush

» Wide-tooth comb

» Close set tooth comb

» Dog toenail clippers

» Short and long, sharp hair scissors

You should ideally groom every day to keep him looking his best. At the very least, three or four times a week to help remove dead hair from your dog's coat. You will find more detailed instructions for grooming your Bichon Frisé in Chapter Seven of this book.

Assortment of Toys – Offering your Bichon Frisé an assortment of toys is very important. Having toys to play with will keep your dog occupied when you are unable to pay attention to him and it will also provide him with something to chew on instead of your furniture and other household items. Different dogs, like different toys, so your best bet is to buy several different kinds and let your dog choose which ones he likes best.

a) Summary of Habitat Requirements

» Indoor/Outdoor: indoor only

» Recommended Accessories: crate, dog bed, food/water dishes, toys, collar, leash, grooming supplies

» Collar and Leash: sized by weight

» Grooming Supplies: wire pin brush/bristle brush, slicker brush, wide-tooth comb fine tooth comb, toenail clippers, scissors.

» Grooming Frequency: brush every day or at least several times a week; professional grooming every 4 to 6 weeks

» Exercise Requirements: daily walk plus playtime

» Crate: highly recommended

» Crate Size: just large enough for dog to lie down and turn around comfortably

» Crate Extras: lined with blanket or plush pet bed

» Food/Water: stainless steel bowls, clean daily

» Toys: start with an assortment, see what the dog likes; include some mentally stimulating toys

3.) Feeding Your Bichon Frisé

In addition to providing your Bichon Frisé with a safe habitat, you also need to give him a healthy diet. The food you choose for your Bichon Frisé will have a direct impact on his health and wellbeing, so do not skimp! It may be tempting to save money by purchasing an inexpensive 'budget' food but you will be robbing your dog of vital nutrients. Skimping on cheap dog food might save you money in the present but it could lead to health problems down the line that might be expensive to treat. In this chapter you will learn the basics about dog nutrition and receive tips for feeding your dog.

a) Nutritional Requirements for Dogs

Just like all living things, dogs require a balance of nutrients in their diet to remain in good health. These nutrients include protein, carbohydrate, fats, vitamins, minerals, and water. Dogs are a carnivorous species by nature so meat plays an important role in their diet, but they do require some carbohydrates as well. Later you will read about the BARF diet. Part of that diet recommends that you feed carbohydrates such as raw fruit and vegetables. This is best served finely chopped, using a food processor or similar. Below you will find an overview of the nutritional needs for dogs in regard to each of the main nutrients. Keep these nutritional requirements in mind when selecting a dog food formula for your Bichon Frisé.

Protein

This nutrient is composed of amino acids and it is essential as a source of energy as well as the growth and development of tissues, cells, organs, and enzymes in your dog's body. It is particularly important for puppy growth, but when the dog reaches maturity, protein is only necessary for maintenance. When the bitch is pregnant and whilst she is feeding pups, she will also need extra protein. Protein can be obtained from both animal and plant-based sources, but animal-based proteins are the most biologically valuable for your dog. There are two categories of amino acids; essential and non-essential. Non-essential amino acids are those that your dog's body is capable of producing. Essential amino acids are those that cannot be produced by the dogs body and therefore he must get this from his diet. The most important essential amino acids for a dog include lysine, arginine, phenylalanine, histidine, methionine, valine, tryptophan, leucine, threonine, and isoleucine.

The quality of the protein can therefore be determined by what extent it contains these essential amino acids. The quality can also be indicated by how well the dog digests the protein. Commercially processed dog foods that contain high levels of cereals are generally considered to contain poor quality protein. The problem is that these products can indicate relatively high levels of protein, but the type of protein contains low if non-existent sources of essential amino acids. Good quality protein would be found in dairy produce such as milk and cheese also eggs and obviously meat.

Protein deficiency would cause all sorts of problems and generally have a serious debilitating effect on the body. Examples of diseases would include, immune deficiency, poor bone growth and muscle development etc. Adult dogs would be greatly affected, but imagine the devastating effects to growing pups.

Again, this is a common problem with poor commercially processed or homemade diets that are either badly designed or contain poor quality cereals.

In the same way that a protein deficiency will cause problems so will an over consumption. The main problems with over feeding protein involve kidney disease. Growing pups and lactating mothers require almost twice as much as an adult dog. The actual percentage of good quality protein for an adult dog would be approximately 8 to 10%, and a lactating bitch and growing pups about 18 to 20%.

Feral dogs, or wolves in the wild, would unlikely be eating high levels of protein on a daily basis. A raw meaty bones diet for example, would make up approximately 60% of their diet

Carbohydrate

The main role of carbohydrates in your dog's diet is to provide energy and dietary fibre. Dogs do not have a minimum carbohydrate requirement but they do need a certain amount of glucose to fuel essential organs like the brain. Carbohydrates are derived from plant sources and are either soluble or insoluble. Soluble consist of simple sugars mostly found in fruit, as well as sugar cane etc. Insoluble carbohydrates, complex or starches as they are otherwise known, originate from vegetables and grains for example leafy veg, potatoes, corn, pumpkin, beans, peas etc. Vegetables as carbohydrates that we feed to our dogs should be raw and fresh. I hasten to add 'vegetables' and not produce such as corn, rice, wheat etc, or products such as pasta. The vegetables should also be processed, finely chopped or crushed, for greater digestion and therefore absorption. Carbohydrates have featured as a significant ingredient in processed dog food. But in a natural sense, carbohydrates are not as important to dogs as it is for humans as a source of energy. Dogs should not be given large amounts of carbohydrate over a prolonged period. Their internal workings are not designed to handle significant amount of this type of food source.

Fibre

Fibre is also an important component of carbohydrates, which isn't ingested but aids greatly with the internal workings. Fibre is also either soluble or insoluble. Soluble basically means that it absorbs water; swells and bulks up to a gelatinous matter. Examples include; oatmeal, apples, beans etc. Insoluble fibres do not absorb water, but act as a bulking agent. Although stating the obvious, insoluble fibre is pretty much parts of vegetable matter that do not absorb water, such as the skins. They act to slow down digestion, aid greater absorption and make the stools easier to pass.

A dog's body is only capable of digesting certain kinds of carbohydrate and too much fibre in the diet is not good for them. It is usually recommended that a mixture of fast and slow fermenting fibres are best. The reason being that too much slow fermenting fibre such as cellulose is likely to cause a sluggish digestion. Bran is considered a good source of fast fermenting fibre but too much could cause diarrhea. Somewhere in the middle is a moderately fermentable fibre such as beet pulp which is a common ingredient in dog foods.

Fats

This is the most highly concentrated form of energy so it is an important part of your dog's diet. Fats provide your dog with twice the energy of protein and carbohydrates. Fats are also important for providing structure for cells and for producing certain types of hormones. They are also necessary to ensure that your dog's body can absorb fat-soluble vitamins. Your dog needs a balance of omega-3 and omega-6 fatty acids in his body and it is best if these fats come from animal-based sources instead of plant-based sources.

Again fat is the best energy food source, but the consumption of fat depends on the lifestyle of the dog. All dogs need some fat. But a sedentary, house dog will obviously need far less than a working dog or feral dog or wolf, who are dependent on food for survival. Too much fat, in the case of a house dog, would lead to obesity, high cholesterol and other diseases, possibly leading to death.

On a more positive note, fat is essential for providing insulation for the body as well as protecting the nerves. It facilitates absorption of vitamins A, K, D and E. In essence, fat is a vital component of every cell in the dogs body. It is important to note that like other food elements, fat has to be provided in the diet.

Essential fatty acids are especially vital for the correct functioning of the dogs body. Without this, the dog will develop a whole host of diseases. It is also important to note that not all fats are recommended. There is a big difference between 'Essential fatty acids' and 'Non-essential fatty acids'.

There is a hormone called 'prostaglandins', which plays an essential role in regulating all bodily functions. Prostaglandins are formulated using essential fatty acids. If essential fatty acids are absent, then non essential fatty acids are utilized, and this results in an imbalance, malfunction and disease.

Essential fatty acids are the types of healthy fats we are told to eat such as omega rich 3, 6 and 9 fish oils. Chicken and pork fat, or lard, are surprisingly excellent sources of essential fatty acid, that may not be healthy for human consumption, but are excellent for dogs.

Non essential acids consist of fats such as beef or mutton suet.

On the next page is a table giving the saturated, monounsaturated and polyunsaturated values for 100g of beef, pork and chicken.

Again, chicken and pork fat are considered excellent sources of 'essential fatty acids'. Animal fat is generally saturated fat that is considered bad for human consumption. The table above indicates that beef, chicken and pork fat have similar lev-

(Values for 100g of beef, chicken and pork fat)

Beef Fat	Chicken Fat	Pork Fat
100 g	100 g	100 g
Saturated 42 g	Saturated 30 g	Saturated 32g
Monounsaturated 50 g	Monounsaturated 21 g	Monounsaturated 21 g
Polyunsaturated 4 g	Polyunsaturated 45 g	Polyunsaturated 11 g

els of saturated fat. But look at the monounsaturated amount for beef. Chicken and Pork are the same and relatively low, but beef is over twice as much. Also notice the very low polyunsaturated amount for beef at only 4 g. Pork fat is almost 3 times as much and chicken fat is over 11 times as much.

Fats that are considered very healthy for human consumption include Olive oil and Canola or rapeseed oil. However, these are very rich in Monounsaturated fats, which if fed to dogs to any great extent would cause an essential fatty acid deficiency. Other oils high in monounsaturated fats include: Peanut oil, sunflower oil, hydrogenated soybean oil, palm oil etc. Polyunsaturated fats are therefore considered to be of greater value to dogs than monounsaturated.

Other than pork and chicken fat, other excellent sources of 'essential fatty acids' include polyunsaturated rich oils such as corn oil, flaxseed/ linseed oil, soybean oil (however, be careful that the soybean oil is not hydrogenated. Hydrogenation is a process that effectively changes soybean and other oils from polyunsaturated to monounsaturated.)

Safflower oil is also recommended as an excellent source of polyunsaturated fatty acid. However, be careful with Safflower oil, as there are two types, one is high in monounsaturated fatty acid and low in polyunsaturated, this is known as (oleic acid). The other high in polyunsaturated fatty acid and low in monounsaturated, known as (linoleic acid).

So to summarise, excellent sources of essential fatty acids include chicken and pork fat, and polyunsaturated rich vegetable oils. Fats to avoid include beef fat (tallow), mutton fat etc , and vegetable oils rich in monounsaturated fatty acids.

Omega 6 Fatty Acid

These are essential fatty acids that are found in pig and poultry fat, as well as many sources of vegetable oil. Many of the commercially processed dog foods as well as home cooked foods based on beef and cooked grain, are likely to be lacking in these fatty acids. As you know, a lack of these essential fatty acids. results in a number of diseases for our dogs such as skin disease, reproduction and growth problems. High levels of Omega 6 fatty acid are found in the following list in descending order of potency; corn oil, cotton seed oil, un-hydrogenated soybean oil, linoleic sunflower oil, peanut oil. Also present, but to a lesser level of Omega 6 are flaxseed oil, olive oil, palm oil, rapeseed (canola) oil.

Omega 3

These important fatty acids are mainly found in fish oils and fish. They largely benefit the brain and nerve functions, so can affect vision, brain activity and fertility in males etc. Flaxseed/linseed oil, is particularly high in Omega 3 and to a significant but lesser extent, canola (rapeseed)oil and soybean. All other oils have omega 3, but to a smaller degree. As linseed/flaxseed is particularly potent, it will be tempting to use this. However, be very careful to only use linseed/flaxseed intended for animal or human consumption. The type available from DIY stores, intended to treat timber and make putty soft etc, is poisonous to dogs and should never be given to them. Also be very careful about giving your dogs fish oils as there is a risk of over dosing their supply of vitamins A and D. If in doubt avoid feeding fish oils.

Have a look at the following source link which gives a vast array of sources, flaxseed and fish oils being the highest:

http://nutritiondata.self.com/foods-000140000000000000000.html

Rich mammalian sources of omega 3 include; eyes and brains etc. Most meats are quite low, but rabbit and lambs liver are considered the best sources.

When supplementing your dogs diet with omega 3 and 6 fatty acids, always ensure to supplement with vitamin E also. Without the presence of vitamin E, these essential fatty acids have a tendency to go off and become rancid in the dogs body.

If you were looking for an oil with a good balance, corn oil and soybean oil are generally considered the best to combine both omega 6 and 3.

The Importance Of Vitamins.

Vitamins – Your dog's body is incapable of producing most vitamins, so it is essential that he get them through his diet. Some of the most important vitamins for dogs include vitamin A, vitamin D, vitamin E and vitamin C.

Sufficient dietary minerals can be obtained from natural sources such as raw meaty bones and the veg, eggs, dairy products mentioned previously. There does seem to be a problem in this regard with processed foods, in that dogs can potentially receive far more minerals than they need. However, vitamins do have a tendency to be lacking in certain processed formulas, and therefore supplementation should be considered. Vitamins are vital for the correct functioning of the body and its many organs. A lack of certain vitamins will lead to diseases.

We typically know vitamins by their letters of the alphabet, A, B, C, D etc. If certain vitamins are absent, then deficiency diseases are bound to manifest. If the dog is getting just enough vitamins, then they will not necessarily show signs of obvious disease, but they are not really at an optimum healthy level. When vitamins are in abundance, then they not only prevent deficiency diseases, but act as a defence against disease. So an abundance promotes health, resists disease, greatly aids reproduction and basically allows the dog to have long term fitness and stamina against stress. In essence, an abundance of vitamins helps all the bodily functions to work efficiently to their optimum level. However, this does not mean that vitamins should be administered at higher unlimited levels. It is possible for an overdose or toxic level to be reached with certain vitamins such as A or D. For severe illness such as with cancer, quite often high doses of vitamin C are administered to combat the disease. Vitamin C and B for example are relatively safe to administer in this way.

Commercially produced dog food is at risk of lacking essential vitamins for a variety of reasons. Dog food is often made up of cheap fillers such as grain and animal by-products and then cooked at high temperatures. What little vitamin value that was present in its raw state is likely to be destroyed or greatly diminished during the cooking process. Vitamins can also be destroyed when mixed with minerals. We will talk more about this later. Also, vitamins that are exposed to air have a limited shelf life. So if dry dog food is not kept in an air tight container it will quickly deteriorate.

The exact same problem can occur if you home cook food for your dog. With the best will in the world, you can use a variety of top quality ingredients but during the cooking process many vitamins can be destroyed. In these cases, vitamins would need to be added back or supplemented. This would be more important during old age, puppy growth or stages of reproduction or lactation.

What Are Vitamins

Vitamins comprise of water soluble and fat soluble. Examples of water soluble are vitamin C and B complex. Vitamins A, D, E and K are classified as fat soluble.

To a certain extent, water soluble vitamins are stored by the body, despite the contrary opinion that they must be supplied on a daily basis. As mentioned previously they can also be given at much higher doses than are recommended. There would be little point in giving high doses that are likely to be excreted, but a dose similar to a human dose would probably be adequate. Again, any that is not immediately used or stored is simply urinated out of the body. It is perfectly safe for the dog and no harm is done.

B Complex

They are extremely important for processing fats, proteins and carbohydrates and turning them into energy. This energy is vital for all bodily functions, for the general purpose of daily activity and for growth. A dog given sufficient Vitamin B would be full of life, bright and energetic, would generally be fit and look fit and healthy. The dog deficient would be totally the opposite, so lacking energy, dull, and overweight. They also play a vital role with the nervous system. Again a deficiency would indicate a nervous dog, whereas sufficient levels would indicate a calm, happy dog.

Similar to humans, a lack of the B complex vitamins can seriously affect the nervous system. It can also have a serious effect on the body during stressful periods. It can also have a significant effect on the energy levels of the dog. The B vitamins are usually administered all together as a complex rather than given separately, unless there is an obvious singular B Vitamin deficiency.

Other problems include:

- » Under development
- » Deficient immune system
- » Production of antibodies is diminished
- » Lack of antioxidants
- » Thymus gland problems
- » Lack of anti aging
- » Tissue degeneration
- » Free radicals are not eliminated from the body
- » More prone to stress
- » Problems with blood production, reproduction, tissue repair, growth.
- » Skin and fur problems occur

In essence they are vital for all bodily functions. They are vital for the health and wellbeing of our dogs at all stages of life.

Rich Food Sources Of B Complex Include:

The best sources of B complex as a whole are liver and brewers yeast. Brewers yeast is often recommended as an excellent source of B complex vitamins. It is also a good source of protein. But other B vitamins, not the full B complex, are present in foods such as brown rice, wholemeal bread, meat, eggs, offal, dairy produce, green leafy veg etc.

Vitamin C

The same rules apply to vitamin C as the above information on the B complex. They are stored by the body to an extent. Can be administered safely at high doses, albeit any not taken up by the body or immediately used, would be eliminated through the urine. Dogs do produce their own vitamin C to an extent, which leads some people to assert they do not need any additional. However, although opinions differ, it is best to give extra in order to ensure your dog is at optimum health. Dogs in the wild would still be eating a lot of vitamin C rich food, and probably to a greater extent than a lot of domestically fed dogs, who are reliant on receiving all their nutrients from commercial food.

Unlike humans who cannot make or store Vitamin C, dogs actually produce this in their liver. However, during times of stress or ill health they would require probably more than the body can naturally produce. Apart from stress and perhaps over work problems can occur relative to reproduction or for the growth of pups.

Vitamin C promotes the following:

» Helps eliminate toxins

» Fights infection and generally boosts the immune system

» Heavily involved in the healing of wounds etc

» Greatly alleviates the stresses of reproduction, lactation, weaning

» Essential for collagen production and other growth factors

» Generally boosts the body in relation to wear and tear associated with exercise and body rejuvenation. Also greatly helps with the aging process

Again as with the B complex, this vitamin is not necessarily dangerous in high doses. However, excess vitamin C, can cause diarrhoea. Again this is not dangerous and a reduction in dosage clears the problem.

Although vitamin C is widely available in a lot of fruit and veg etc, some people also like to add a supplement also. This can be in line with what you may supplement yourself, and a general guideline is to add up to 100 milligrams per kilo. So if your dog weighs 10kg then a 1 gram or 1000 mg tablet could be given. That isn't to say that you should administer that dose regardless. Also please take into account fluctuations in stress levels. A relatively stress free dog would be fine on up to 100mg per kg. if your dog was under heavy stress such as over work, or lactation and weaning then this could be increased to about 300mg per kg. It is also advisable to split the daily dose given. So give 100mg in two separate doses of 50mg. if it were 300mg administered, then split this into 6 separate doses and so on.

'Bowel Tolerance' is a gauge as to whether your dog is receiving too much vitamin C, which is indicated by diarrhoea

If a dog is predominantly feeding on a raw diet, i.e. raw meaty bones along with vegetables and other ingredients, then only a minimum supplement of up to 100mg per kg, would be needed.

Under normal healthy conditions it will not matter a great deal what type of vitamin C your dog receives.

Vitamin C is known as ascorbic acid, but be aware that there are different forms such as calcium ascorbate, ester C and sodium ascorbate. It is important to know this because if for example your dog suffers with hip dysplasia calcium ascorbate should not be given, because of the extra calcium. A dog with heart disease should not be given sodium ascorbate, due to the sodium.

Fat Soluble Vitamins

Vitamins A, E and K have anti ageing/antioxidant properties. Vitamin D and A, in particular should never be given at high doses as they are extremely toxic at high levels. The other problem is that unlike B and C vitamins, these are stored to a greater extent in the body. The effect of topping up, again can potentially build up to toxic levels. Having said that, despite the dangers of toxic overload, all of these vitamins should never be allowed to become non-existent as diseases will arise as a result of the deficiency.

Vitamin A, is vital for most if not all of the bodily processes. It is particularly important for sight, immune system functioning, mucous membranes, skin, adrenal glands, reproduction, growth etc. To supplement with Vitamin A an amount of between 100 to 200 iu per kg, would be safe. So a 20 kg dog would not need more than 200 x 20 = 4000iu per day. If however, you were feeding your dog liver once or twice per week it is unlikely you would need any extra supplementation.

Do check any commercial food levels of vitamin A. The likely hood is that there will be just enough, but not necessarily enough to keep the dog at optimum health. Usually commercial feed will be about 50 to 100iu per kg per day.

I would never recommend attempting to give the maximum non toxic level until you are sure what you are doing. Give smaller doses initially and if you see significant general improvement then gradually increase this per month. It is also a good idea initially to supplement for one month and then don't give anything the following month, then restart again.

Once again, feeding liver once or twice per week may be safer until you get experience and always monitor how your dog is doing.

When should you never supplement vitamin A?

Never supplement a dog with vitamin A if they have liver or kidney disease. Once again, if the diet is already rich in vitamin A, for instance if liver is regularly given, then again do not add any vitamin A supplement.

It is useful to know that where cases of toxicity and overdose occur, this has been when up to 100 times the recommended limits have been administered and usually for prolonged periods. The general opinion is that up to 10 times the recommended dose would be safe. Again, if this level of up to 10 times was exceeded for a short period of time, it is unlikely to cause any serious effects.

Signs of toxicity

The following list will give you some idea of abnormalities that can occur from overdosing Vitamin A

- » Cartilage degeneration
- » Internal bleeding
- » Blood that doesn't clot easily
- » Weight loss
- » Appetite loss
- » Enteritis
- » Hereditary abnormalities
- » Fractures
- » Malformed bones
- » Thickened skin
- » conjunctivitis
- » Red blood cell count reduction
- » Liver and kidney malfunction
- » suppressed keratinisation

What do the μg and iu symbols mean?

if you are not familiar with the μg symbol, it means micro-gram and can also be written as mcg. To give you some comparative values, 1 milligram = 1,000 μg, 1 gram = 1,000,000 μg,

Again, you may see food sources measured as IU, which stands for International Unit.

Whilst μg is obviously a quantifiable unit of weight, it is not as easy to quantify and therefore compare μg with its equivalent IU. So it is not simply a matter of saying 1 IU = X amount of μg.

Whereas μg, is simply the mass or weight, a substances IU is measured in terms of concentration of potency. So in other words, 2 exact same substances for example may have concentrations of 100 mg and 300 mg respectively. It's the same thing but one is obviously more potent than the other. This occurs very often with herbal supplements. There are many products available for Echinacea for example. You will see several products with 30 tablets for example, sold for the different prices. It is only when you delve deeper and look at the % or mg of potency that you realise why.

So taking some examples from the following link; https://en.wikipedia.org/wiki/Vitamin_A. if you scroll down the page of that site, you will see a large list of food sources in μg. But if you search for similar food sources on the following site, you will see similar food sources in IU; http://www.healthaliciousness.com/articles/food-sources-of-vitamin-A.php

I think it is fair to say that cod liver oil is one of the richest sources of vitamin A, as the Wikipedia list confirms this at 30000 μg. But if you take sweet potato for example, on the Wikipedia site it is measured as 961 μg per 100 grams. On the Healthaliciousness site however, sweet potato, which is incidentally rated as one of, if not the most potent vegetable source of vitamin A, is stated as 19218IU per 100 grams, but also states its 'retinol' amount as 961 µg.

But please do not make the mistake of doing a simple calculation of dividing 19218 by 961 = 19.99792. Therefore concluding that 1 IU = 19.99792 µg as this would be incorrect. You will be able to calculate this way and get some surprisingly accurate figures. Take carrot for example, with 835 µg. If we multiply that by 19.99792 we get 16,698 and the actual IU is 17,033, so quite close. You could also take cantaloupe melon whose actual IU is 3382, and if you take its µg of 169 and multiply that by 19.99792 you get 3380, which is very accurate. But if you take mango whose µg is 38 and multiply that by 19.99792 you get 760, when its actual IU is 1082, so quite a bit of a difference there. All I would say is that it is possible to use this as a way to calculate some food sources, but I personally wouldn't want to rely on it as a definite way to convert in all cases.

The following list are examples of Vitamin A sources, in this case from Wikipedia: These are in order of potency.

» cod liver oil (30000 µg)

» liver (turkey) (8058 µg)

» liver (beef, pork, fish) (6500 µg)

» liver (chicken) (3296 µg)

» sweet potato (961 µg)

» carrot (835 µg)

» broccoli leaf (800 µg) please note there is a big difference between leaf and florets with broccoli florets only being (31 µg)

» kale (681 µg)

obviously there are many more examples but these are the most common with high potency of vitamin A.

All of the above are highly recommended sources for dogs, but for obvious reasons be very careful with cod liver oil as they are far more potent than the others and therefore a greater risk of toxicity. Other recommended sources are all other green leaf veg, corn, pumpkin and squash etc.

Vitamin A Deficiency – Vitamin A as you know,is a type of fat-soluble vitamin that comes from liver, dairy, and certain yellow vegetables. This vitamin is essential for the healthy formation of bones and teeth. It also plays a role in healthy skin, coat, and eyesight. A deficiency in Vitamin A may cause poor growth and development, skin problems, poor coat quality, eye problems, and immune problems. These deficiencies would be more problematic with dry food as apposed to canned.

Vitamin E

Vitamin E is a fat-soluble vitamin that plays a role in metabolizing fats and supporting healthy cell function; it is also a type of antioxidant. Sources of vitamin E include liver, vegetable oil, wheat germ, and leafy green vegetables. A deficiency of vitamin E can lead to reproductive disorders as well as disorders of the liver, heart, muscle, nerves, and eyes. It can also have a negative impact on your dog's bowels.

Free radicals that are present throughout your dogs body, pose a real problem in terms of cancer, premature ageing, arthritis, strokes etc. Free radicals are actually formed in the dogs fat tissues, and if left to sit there, can go rancid. Vitamin E, otherwise known as an antioxidant, is the best antidote for these free radicals.

Vitamin E combats so many problems that can affect your dog. Examples of this are; arresting premature ageing. Helping to prevent heart disease, blood clots that cause strokes. Acting as a barrier to disease, toxic heavy metals. Greatly aiding reproduction and energy production as well as producing vitamin C. Vitamin E is also necessary to help fight infection.

Vitamin E is also greatly needed if oils such as linseed oil, corn oil, sunflower oil, cod liver oil among others, are a significant part of your dogs diet. The major reason revolves around vitamin E preventing fat rancidity. When dogs ingest these types of polyunsaturated oils there is a risk they will go rancid, and vitamin E is the answer to make sure this doesn't happen. It is important to know that whilst vitamin E combats the effects of fat rancidity, the process of combating actually kills the vitamin E. So although it does the job your dog needs, it obviously needs replenishing. So feeding lots of polyunsaturated oil, without sufficient vitamin E in the system, will eventually lead to a deficiency and resulting disease.

It is recommended a 25kg dog for example, receives between 1 mg and 5 mg of Vitamin E per day

As we know 1 mg = 1000 µg (mcg), so if we want to find out the equivalent for 1 kg use the following;

A 25kg dog needs 1 to 5 mg, so that is 1000 µg to 5000 µg. So if we divide 1000 µg by 25kg we get 40 µg. So 1 kg = 40 µg. Do the same calculation for 5000 µg to get 200 µg.

So work out your dogs daily requirement by multiplying its weight in kg by between 40 µg and 200 µg. So again 25 x 40 is 1000 and 25 x 200 is 5000. If your dog weighs 10 kg then 10 x 40 is 400 µg and 10 x 200 is 2000 µg. So it is recommended that your dog receives between 40 and 200 µg per kilo of your dogs weight. Please note that these amounts would give your dog an adequate supply, not necessarily an optimum level, or even a toxic level. Once again, if your dog was receiving Vitamin E within those bounds recommended, please remember that they would need more if fish oils or polyunsaturated vegetable oils were regularly given.

Usually in this case it is recommended to supplement between 10 and 20 mg per day per kg of your dogs weight. So for a 10 kg dog, a safe dosage would be, 100 to 200 mg per day.

Sources For Vitamin E

High levels of vitamin E are found in dark leafy greens. They are also found in the polyunsaturated fats mentioned as causing a problem with rancidity. These are wheatgerm oil, cottonseed, safflower, soybean etc. It may sound paradoxical, but although they have reasonably high levels of vitamin E, it only becomes a problem when the fat starts to go rancid. When this happens, as previously mentioned the vitamin E, counteracts this but in the process, dies off and so causing a deficiency.

Liver, eggs, certain grains as well as dairy produce are other good sources

Toxic Side Effects

Immediate large doses can cause temporary high blood pressure, but vitamin E is not known to cause any significant problems or side effects. Of course this does not mean you should administer large doses for the sake of it.

Vitamin D

You probably already know this as the sunshine vitamin, sunbathing or just spending short periods of time in direct sunlight, provides our bodies with vitamin D. However, if it is a cloudy day or the area is affected with airborne pollutants, mist, smoke etc, then the effects are greatly diminished and supplementation would be needed. The same goes for our dogs. It is thought that 10 to 15 minutes of 'direct' sunlight would provide our dogs with their 'recommended' daily dose.

Vitamin D plays an important function by aiding absorption of phosphorus and calcium. It also regulates the depositing and if need be, the withdrawing of calcium and phosphorus from the bones.

The main issue as to whether the dog is receiving enough vitamin D revolves around how much direct sunlight they are exposed to per day. If the dog is fed a meaty bones, BARF diet, and is exposed to even a small amount of sun per day, they will not need any supplementation. If that isn't the case, then they will probably need some form of supplementing.

Cod liver oil has always been seen as one of, if not the best source for vitamin D, but all the fish liver oils contain good amounts of vitamin D. Fish such as herring, catfish, salmon, trout, mackerel, sardine etc are also great sources.

Toxic Effects

Vitamin D is similar to vitamin A in that much care is needed to ensure your dog does not receive too much. One of the main problems involves calcium and the possibility that too much calcium is deposited in the body. This in turn can cause abnormal bodily functioning.

Recommended Amounts

Vitamin D is particularly important for growing puppies as a deficiency can result in bone diseases such as rickets. If you notice a poor appetite and therefore poor growth and weight loss, then a deficiency of vitamin D could be the problem. Bone problems will be evident such as fractures, malformed or misshaped bones, enlarged joints etc.

The recommended daily dose for growing puppies per kilo body weight is 22 iu. It is suggested however, that that up to 100 iu per kg is a safe level. So a 4 kg puppy at this level can safely take 400 iu per day. As an example, the 450ml bottle of 'Seven Seas' cod liver oil that I have, suggests that 10ml (2 tea spoons) of oil contains 400 iu of vitamin D. However it also states that the same 10ml (2 tea spoons) would provide 4000 iu of vitamin A, which for a puppy would be a toxic level. So please be very careful with supplementing a puppies intake of fish oil such as cod liver oil. In this case, you could still give the puppy cod liver oil, but taking into consideration their recommended vitamin A limits. Also, be aware that potencies of cod liver oil supplies vary. Again check the 'iu' equivalent on the bottle as some may be stronger than others.

Deficiencies of vitamin D may well arise in dogs on a bad diet of poor quality commercially processed food, dogs predominantly fed meat, older dogs that have difficulty manufacturing vitamin D or even lack of sunlight.

Vitamin K

Vitamin K has a variety of health promoting uses. It is particularly important as a blood clotting agent, as well as growth, reproduction, healthy skin, anti ageing properties and as an antioxidant. There is an interesting connection with vitamin K and faeces, as vitamin K is produced in the large intestine, by bacteria which is then passed into the faeces of most animals. So if you see your dog eating another animals faeces, it could well be an indication of a vitamin K deficiency. It may not be, but at least you know that they are actually getting nutritional benefits such as an intake of vitamin K. Incidentally feces can provide high levels of protein, fatty acids, vitamins including B, K, antioxidants, minerals and fibre. Dogs that eat feces may be indicating a lack of nutrients in their diet. But again, please do not automatically assume this is the case. I have known two dogs that were fed exactly the same diet and were both in excellent condition and yet one would regularly eat horse feces whilst out on walks. This was never a significant amount. The dog in question would also stop at every puddle she passed and drink out of water containers left for horses. She could well be getting some mineral benefit but rightly or wrongly it was assumed she was one of those dogs that likes to pick at and taste anything.

Other sources of vitamin K are dark green leafy vegetables such as kale, chard, spinach etc and other vegetables such as salad veg, brassica veg etc. Liver and fish are also good sources.

Vitamin K Toxicity

Natural vitamin K is actually non toxic, and it is unlikely your dog will eat enough natural foods in a day to cause an over load. However synthetically manufactured vitamin K can be toxic in high doses. Very high doses of over 100 times the recommended daily dose are likely to have a toxic effect. The recommended amount is up to 1 mg per kg of body weight.

Once again, providing your dog is receiving a BARF type diet with plenty of raw meaty bones, vegetables and other food sources, supplementation is unlikely.

Minerals – Minerals are a type of inorganic compound that cannot by synthesized and thus must come from your dog's diet. The most important minerals for dogs include calcium, phosphorus, Magnesium, Selenium, potassium, sodium, copper, zinc, and iron. Minerals are particularly important for developing and maintaining strong bones and teeth. Other ,

The two most important minerals for a dogs health, particularly the growing pup, and generally breeding and reproduction, are phosphorus and calcium. The main natural source of these in terms of a dogs diet are found in raw (not cooked) bones. As well as calcium and phosphorus, bones are also likely to store copper, chromium, iodine, iron, magnesium, manganese, potassium, selenium, strontium, zinc etc.

Dr. Ian Billinghurst, states in Give Your Dog a Bone

Do realise your dog will not, cannot, suffer mineral deficiencies, imbalances or excesses, when raw meaty bones make up the bulk of its diet. This applies to dogs of all ages, including puppies. And I don't just mean puppies of the smaller breeds: I mean all breeds of puppies, including most definitely the giant breeds.

An imbalance of any essential vitamin, mineral or other element can obviously have major health consequences. But a major problem associated with mineral imbalance isn't necessarily a deficiency, but an over dose. Too much calcium can result in the calcium combining with other essential minerals such as zinc, iron, copper etc, and preventing the absorption of the zinc, iron, copper etc. This in turn would set up a deficiency of the zinc, iron, copper etc

Too much sodium or salt can result in cardiovascular disease and hypertension. An excess of phosphorus can lead to diseases such as kidney failure. All of these problems can be the result of feeding dogs either poor quality commercial dog food, or over supplementation.

Problems With Supplementation

Be very careful about supplementing in isolation. Calcium seems to be a big culprit of diseases and disorders for both growing pups as well as adult dogs. But because it is well known that calcium can negate other minerals, there is a temptation to supplement these other minerals such as zinc, copper and iron. There can be all manner of skin, skeletal growth and arthritic conditions associated with this kind of mineral imbalance. In fact any mineral that is supplemented in isolation can cause an overdose, imbalance and resulting disorder or disease.

Problems With Blood Tests Etc To Establish Deficiencies

Establishing a nutritional deficiency via a blood test should not be relied on as conclusive. The following link to an article highlighting this, indicates that certain blood tests have revealed no deficiency in particular diets. But after further investigation a serious deficiency has been diagnosed and successfully treated: http://www.petmd.com/blogs/thedailyvet/ktudor/2013/nov/why-blood-tests-are-not-good-for-testing-nutritional-status-in-pets-31029

Of course blood tests and other testing can in certain cases, be the most efficient way of diagnosing a problem. But again, where diet is concerned it is usually a question of elimination of symptoms and possible causes.

Water

Water is the most important nutrient for all animals. Your dog would be able to survive for a while without food if he had to, but he would only last a few days without water. Water accounts for as much as 70% of your dog's bodyweight and even a 10% decrease in your dog's body water levels can be very dangerous. Provide your Bichon Frisé with plenty of fresh water at all times.

It is common knowledge that tap water is processed using a number of chemicals and there is much debate as to possible links to cancer. Obviously the reasons for this chemical processing are to kill bacteria present in its raw state at sewage plants etc. Many people are now filtering tap water as a way to purify this tap water as much as possible. This is also a good idea for dogs. As you will regularly see dogs drinking out of puddles, another good idea is to try and recycle rain water. Admittedly in areas of pollution, there is a risk of acid rain etc, but there is a good chance that rain water will contain fewer potentially harmful chemicals than tap water.

b) The Importance of Diet – Nutritional Deficiencies

Although we cover diet in the feeding section, it is included here from a health, disease and deficiency point of view. As well as vitamin deficiencies mentioned above we will touch on mineral deficiencies here.

If you do not provide your dog with a healthy diet, his body will not be able to function as it should, and he may be more likely to develop illnesses and infections. In addition to providing your dog with high-quality dog food, you also need to make sure that his diet provides certain nutrients. Dogs are prone to developing certain nutritional deficiencies which can produce some very real and dangerous symptoms.

Some of the nutritional deficiencies to which your Bichon Frisé is most likely to be prone may include:

» General malnutrition

» Vitamin A deficiency

- Magnesium deficiency
- Iron deficiency anemia
- Vitamin E deficiency
- Calcium deficiency

General Malnutrition – Malnutrition is defined as the imbalanced, excessive, or insufficient consumption of nutrients. Some of the signs of malnutrition include an emaciated appearance, poor skin and coat quality, bad breath, swollen gums, abnormal stools, growth problems, poor immunity, lack of energy, and behavioral problems.

Magnesium Deficiency – Magnesium and potassium are the most abundant substances in cells, so a magnesium deficiency can be very serious. Magnesium is required for most metabolic functions and in the development of healthy bones and tissue. Symptoms of magnesium deficiency include weakness, trembling, depression, behavioral changes, and loss of coordination. Careful treatment for this deficiency is essential because too much magnesium can be fatal for your dog.

Iron Deficiency "Anemia" – Iron is required to produce and develop red blood cells and those blood cells help to carry oxygen throughout your dog's body. A deficiency of iron can lead to anemia, a condition in which your dog doesn't have enough healthy red blood cells to carry oxygen to organs and muscles. Symptoms of iron deficiency anemia include loss of appetite, decreased growth, lethargy/weakness, depression, rapid breathing, and dark-colored stools.

Calcium Deficiency – Your dog requires a delicate balance of calcium and phosphorus to maintain healthy bones and teeth. Calcium is also important for nerve, heart and muscle function as well as blood clotting. A calcium deficiency can lead to spasms, lameness, heart palpitations, anxiety, bone fractures, arthritis, high blood pressure, and more. This type of deficiency is often caused by a high-meat diet because meat is very high in phosphorus. This can lead to an imbalance of phosphorus and calcium.

Additional Problems with calcium excess

Dried food has been more of a problem of calcium excess, with some cases showing up to a dozen times the amount actually needed. Obviously from a growth point of view calcium is a vital nutrient. However, in excess the calcium not absorbed by the body is eventually excreted in the feces. The problem, as you have already learned, is that calcium combines with other essential minerals such as zinc and results in the zinc not being absorbed by the body. However, as well as zinc, copper and iron are affected in the same way which can result in anaemia. Where zinc deficiency occurs, the aforementioned problems associated with skin diseases, stunted growth in pups, reproductive and immunity problems are likely to manifest. In addition wounds take longer to heal, the nervous system is affected, bone abnormalities occur, testicular growth is affected, the thyroid gland doesn't function properly, the body loses protein, etc. To say the least, the results of a zinc deficiency are pretty grim.

An excess of calcium is also known to be a contributory factor in dogs suffering with bloat. When the body detects a calcium excess is produces 'gastrin', which is a hormone that thickens the ends of the stomach and makes the expulsion of gases difficult to pass.

So again, in addition to deficiencies in certain vitamins or minerals, dogs can also suffer from an excess of certain nutrients. For example, too much vitamin A can cause your Bichon Frisé's bones to become brittle and his skin to become dry. An excess of vitamin D could cause your dog's bones to become too dense and for his tissue and joints to calcify. Too much vitamin C can lead to kidney stones, excess calcium can lead to phosphorus imbalances, and too much polyunsaturated fat (such as from fish oil) may lead to a vitamin E imbalance.

c) Calorie Requirements for Dogs

Your dog requires a certain number of calories each day in order for his body to maintain proper function. Calorie needs for dogs vary from one breed to another and they also depend on the dog's age, size, sex, and activity level.

Below you will find a chart outlining the basic calorie needs for dogs at different ages:

Calorie Needs For Dogs (Per Day)

Type of Dog	*10 Lbs*	*15 Lbs*	*20 Lbs*
Puppy (Under 4 Months)	*618 Calories*	-	-
Puppy (Over 4 Months)	*412 Calories*	-	-
Normal Adult Dog	*329 Calories*	*438 Calories*	*547 Calories*
Active Adult Dog	*412 Calories*	*548 Calories*	*684 Calories*
Pregnant Female	*618 Calories*	*822 Calories*	*1,026 Calories*
Lactating Female	*824+ Calories*	*1,096+ Calories*	*1,368+ Calories*

The calorie information in the chart above is a basic guideline. Your dog's individual needs may be different. The best way to determine how many calories your Bichon Frisé actually needs is to calculate his Resting Energy Requirement (RER), and to then modify it according to his age and activity level. The formula for calculating your dog's RER is as follows:

RER = 30 x (weight in kg) + 70

For example, if your dog weighed 45 pounds, you would use the following formula: RER = 30 x (45/2.205) +70. So (45/2.205) = 20.40816327, then multiply that by 30 = 612.244898, then add 70 = 682 rounded down to the nearest whole number. You will note that in order to determine your dog's weight in kilograms you need to divide it by 2.205 first. So using our formula and the example given as shown above, a 45-pound dog has an estimated RER of about 682 calories. To determine your dog's daily energy requirements you will need to multiply his RER by a factor that varies by age and activity level. Use the chart on the next page to determine what number to multiply your dog's RER by:

So following on, if we use another example, in this case our 20 Lb dog in the chart, to get to 684 we calculate as follows:

20 divided by 2.205 = 9.070295.
9.070295 x 30 = 272.1088.
272.1088 + 70 = 342.1088

Now taking into consideration the activity level of the dog as light so multiply the RER by 2; we multiply 342.1088 by 2 = 684 rounded to the nearest whole number

Based on the information in the chart on the next page, you can see that puppies and pregnant dogs have much higher calorie needs than adult dogs. When your Bichon Frisé puppy is growing he will need to eat a lot more than he will when he is fully grown. Puppy foods are typically higher in both protein and calories than adult dog foods. This accounts for the needs of growing puppies. In pregnant females you typically do not need to start increasing rations until the last three weeks of gestation. Once the dog gives birth, her calorie needs will increase again so that she can produce enough milk for her puppies. The more puppies in the litter, the higher her calorie needs will be.

When your dog gets older, his calorie needs will drop. Senior dogs typically require 20% fewer calories than younger dogs because their metabolisms slow down and they become less active. Many dogs become overweight as they age because their owners do not reduce their feeding portions to account for changes in metabolism and energy. Once a dog becomes obese it can be difficult for him to lose weight, so be especially careful with your dog's diet once he reaches "senior" level around 7 years of age.

So what is a good diet choice for your Bichon Frisé dog Well you have many options and some dog owners like to mix and match, to keep things interesting for your dog.

d) How to Choose a Healthy Dog Food

Now that you have a basic understanding of your dog's nutritional needs you are ready to learn how to choose a healthy dog food. If you walk down the aisles at your local pet store you could easily be overwhelmed by the sheer number of options you have. Not only are there

Resting Energy Requirements (RER)

Type of Dog	*Daily Calorie needs*
Weight Loss	*1.0 x RER*
Normal Adult (Neutered)	*1.6 x RER*
Normal Adult (Intact)	*1.8 x RER*
Lightly Active Adult	*2.0 x RER*
Moderately Active Adult	*3.0 x RER*
Pregnant (First 42 Days)	*1.8 x RER*
Pregnant (Last 21 Days)	*3.0 x RER*
Lactating Female	*4.8 x RER*
Puppy (2 to 4 Months)	*3.0 x RER*
Puppy (4 to 12 Months)	*2.0 x RER*

many different brands to choose from but most brands offer several different flavors or formulas. In this section you will learn the basics about how to determine whether a commercial dog food is healthy or not.

Commercial Dog Food

The history of commercial dog food goes back to the 1850s when it was first manufactured in England. This product largely consisted of processed bone meal and cereals. Some 30 odd years later U.S. mill owners realised the huge profit potential of taking their by-products and turning it into dog food. In 1922 the first type of canned dog food was produced using horse meat. This basic idea is still used today with a few modifications. In an age where millions are spent on advertising, it is no surprise that commercially produced dog food is the most well known and unfortunately, popular method of feeding our pets.

Do not rule out a great quality dried food mixed with wet food of some type. When you are choosing a commercial food though, keep in mind that less is more. Don't look at the promises on the packaging, but turn it around and look at the ingredients on the back, this will tell you so much more.

If there is anything that you don't recognize don't buy the food until you have found out what the ingredient is. If the main ingredient is some kind of meat followed by the words 'meal' or 'derivatives' don't buy the food.

In our fast paced world were fast food chains flourish and ready meals fill supermarket shelves, it is unsurprising that dogs are fed in the same way. It has to be said, opening a tin of dog food or feeding a few scoops of kibble takes a few minutes of our time. Tinned stuff can be stored anywhere for years and an opened bag of kibble will remain relatively fresh for a month or so. All we need are the food manufacturers to feed us with words such as 'healthy', 'nutritious', 'premium', 'complete', 'balanced diet' and we are sold. I personally have mixed feelings about commercial foods. Again some brands are better than others and if you are pushed for time initially then it can offer an OK temporary alternative. I would not however, recommend this in the long term. I would at the very least incorporate raw natural foods, preferably a permanent BARF diet.

Get Cooking

Your second option is to cook your dog's food at home.

This is actually quite easy and there is no reason why you can't alternate between home prepared dog food and a good quality commercial food. Variety is the spice of life after all, and this applies to dogs too.

A careful mix of sweet potatoes, green leafy veggies, beans and legumes with added white fish or other protein source is a perfect home-made dog's dinner. Adding some type of oil is also good for the coat and the joints. Again, please do read the section on essential fatty acids and the various suitable oils.

If you make a big pot of food at a time and vary the types of carbohydrate and protein, then you should easily meet all of your dog's vitamin and mineral needs over a few weeks recurring.

However, be careful with home cooked food and realise that even though you know what has gone into this food, it may be deficient in certain nutrients. What some people tend to do to be extra sure that they are meeting their dog's nutritional needs is usually along the following lines. They alternate between commercial food and home-made then add a digestive enzyme with vitamin supplement prepared for your dog. Surely the fact that they are having to add a digestive enzyme and vitamin and mineral supplement indicates that the food is deficient in some way.

Why Food Is Cooked

Wild feral dogs and wolves will eat rotten 'contaminated', flesh and bones, other animal feces, animal guts etc. In other words, food that we would consider infected, laden with germs likely to make us ill. But for the dog, these are a rich source of nutrients the dog needs such as enzymes, vitamins, proteins, antioxidants, fatty acids etc. The digestive system of the feral dog is actually no different to the domesticated dog.

We view cooking as necessary as it breaks food down, making it more digestible for humans. Again the digestion of dogs is somewhat different to us, and the digestive system of domestic dogs is actually not dissimilar to its ancestor the wolf.

Many dog owners will assert that they feed their dogs cooked food and the dogs thrive and show no obvious immediate signs of ill health. The point is, the dogs are unlikely to die immediately, but there is a likelihood for them to gradually show signs of ill health and premature aging, resulting in an early death.

The main reason commercially produced dog food is cooked is to kill germs and parasites. Cooking also destroys much of the vitamin content and food therefore loses much of its nutritious value. Furthermore, cooking destroys antioxidants which again combat the effects of aging. Lysine and methionine, two essential amino acids are also thought to be destroyed by the cooking process. Without them, the dogs health in general and resistance to disease is affected. Problems associated with general growth, skin, bones as well as problems associated with pregnancy can also manifest.

The cooking process actually changes the molecular structure of food and affects the digestibility of proteins for dogs. This change results in the food becoming foreign to the body which can cause allergic reactions, indigestion and at worse, be carcinogenic.

Unfortunately, cooking additionally destroys enzymes. Living enzymes naturally break food down until it decays. Cooking kills the enzymes and therefore slows this process down, which means the food can be stored for longer. This is great news for the commercial dog food industry and us the buyer to an extent, but a lot less so for the dogs.

Enzymes present in raw food are proteins which not only aid the digestive system, but actually slow down the aging process. As well as aiding digestion, food enzymes are known to have major health benefits for dogs. These include: as well as anti aging, pancreas functioning, alleviating joint disease and arthritis. Lack of enzymes also contributes to a process known as 'cross linking'. Cross linking is a devastating aging process that contributes to inelastic wrinkled skin, hardened arteries, damaged genes resulting in reproductive problems, birth defects and at worst cancer. Other diseases associated with premature aging include heart disease, kidney disease and arthritis.

It is generally the pancreas which produces enzymes. If sufficient enzymes are present in food, then the pancreas does not have to produce any extra. If the required enzymes are not present, then the pancreas has to work to produce them. If the pancreas is overworked, then certain conditions and diseases can appear such as Pancreatitis and diabetes.

Problems With Home Cooked Dog Food

» Lack of essential fatty acids

» A soft mush and therefore nothing to chew on to promote dental health

» Generally contains rice, pasta or other grain/ cereal

based ingredients and therefore not dissimilar to commercially processed foods

Problems associated with cooking i.e. killing of enzymes, vitamin and mineral degeneration, lack of antioxidants. Again because of the combined stew/cooking, the same problems associated with mineral combination will occur, such as zinc and calcium.

Problems Feeding Table Scraps

In all probability, table scraps are unlikely to represent a complete diet. They are bound to be lacking in essential nutrients such as protein, calcium and other essential vitamins and minerals. They are also likely to be high in meat trimming such as fat or from gravy, and carbohydrates such as vegetables. Of course this sort of diet is likely to be very palatable for the dog, but particularly if high fat sources were given, would quickly lead to obesity. Many vets advocate that whilst perfectly acceptable in moderation and on occasion, table scraps should certainly not represent the bulk of a dogs diet.

Raw Feeding

Over the last few years raw feeding has become increasingly popular and most that try it never go back to cooked food for their pets. Raw feeding is so popular that manufacturers are preparing raw food in the same way as they have been preparing cooked food for years.

The idea behind this feeding type is that the dog's diet is as natural as possible. It is based upon the diet a wild carnivore would eat. Some meat and offal, some bones and green vegetables; all raw are fed to the dog in order to mirror the wild diet. The wild diet would usually have been small prey animals, grass, greens and bones.

Advocates of this feeding type usually state that it is the best decision that they have ever made on behalf of their dog whilst there are very few that turn away from raw feeding after trial-ing it.

There are some precautions to be aware of if you are considering raw feeding though. There have been some links between infection of arthritic joints and raw meat. Similarly too many raw bones can cause digestive blockages. Some experts also believe that our dogs were more scavengers as they developed and ate less meat than we think.

I suggest that if this feeding type is something you may consider, then do a lot of research first. The commercial raw foods are varying in quality much like the commercial cooked dog foods. If you are putting your dog's diet together at home then it's vital to consider varied and balanced nutrition.

If you are changing your dog's food at all then remember to wean gradually from one to the other as a quick change can easily be the cause of stomach upsets.

Barf Diet

The BARF diet (Biologically Appropriate Raw Food Diet) was first developed by veterinarian, Dr.Ian Billinghurst. The BARF diet contains thoroughly ground raw and meaty bones, raw vegetables, raw offal and supplements. You can find these in patty form, which you can break up into bits when feeding your adult Bichon Frisé. Although Dr. Billinghurst suggests it is safe to feed raw meaty bones to growing puppies, some breeders and vets are against the idea, for reasons such as upset stomachs and the need to build them up to such a diet. He does however say in his book 'Give Your Dog A Bone' that he has successfully reared puppies on such a diet. He goes on to say that he would start them on minced chicken wings, bone and all, then soon after give them the whole chicken wing and so on.

If this interests you, please do refer to one of the excellent books I mention below. By the way, I am in no way affiliated or connected to the authors, they are books that many forum contributors recommend and that I have personally read and found useful and inspiring.

Many veterinarians have claimed that this diet helps dogs with skin disorders, which are allergic to grain, preservatives, and other added ingredients found in commercial brands.

There has also been some negative feedback about this diet, such as the threat of SalmonellaandListeria monocytogenes strains. This has been predominantly asserted by the FDA.

I have to say that I am a great believer in feeding raw meaty bones and there have been some excellent studies and books written. As mentioned, Ian Billinghurst an Australian Vet and Nutritionist originally proposed the idea that dogs have become ill and are dying prematurely because they have been deprived of their natural inheritance, 'raw meat and bones'. His books are still available but quite expensive, but his best seller 'Give Your Dog A Bone', is available reasonably cheaply as a Kindle download. The book is excellent and is well worth a read. I have only predominantly fed raw meaty bones and other raw ingredients to adult dogs, but I cannot comment on his assertion that it is perfectly acceptable to feed pups a BARF diet. In my experience, my dogs have not only looked much brighter, fitter and healthier, but their stools are more solid and their breath has been relatively odorless.

Other excellent books covering the subject include: 'Raw Meaty Bones' and 'Work Wonders' both by Dr Tom Lonsdale. 'Raw and Natural Nutrition for Dog, by Lew Olson PhD. Also 'Natural Nutrition for Dogs and Cats' by Kymythy R. Shultze.

I think if I have to sum up the message for BARF, raw meaty bones feeding, it is that you need to ask questions of the whole commercial food industry and that feeding a more natural primitive diet will provide your dog with greater health and longevity. Probably on a par with only buying puppies that come from reputable breeders who health test the parents, I would say nutrition is the other most important consideration regarding the health and happiness of your dog. Of course obedience training and knowledge of your dogs behavior are important aspects for successfully keeping a happy relationship with your new friend. But I believe too much emphasis is placed on 'Dog Whisperers' and their training been the be all and end all. If your dog is not healthy, it will not be happy. Ask yourself the following questions: Would you rather spend a small fortune on regular visits to the vet over the duration of your dogs life? Or would you rather your dog is happy and healthy and destined to live a longer life, with far fewer visits to the vet? Please do consider the BARF diet at whatever stage of life your dog is.

Points to bear in mind with feeding a raw diet.

Chewing raw meat and bones exercises and massages the teeth and gums, above all keeping them clean. If the teeth and gums becomes diseased and infected, they create toxins and bacteria which will be ingested and contribute to ill health.

It is important that you keep any raw food separate from your own, for obvious reasons of cross contamination. This includes thoroughly cleaning surfaces and utensils with hot soapy water and anti-bacterial sprays suitable for food surfaces.

Fresh meat and bones will need refrigerating, but there is nothing to stop you buying in bulk and freezing portions. Any refrigerated food can be kept in seal-able food storage containers.

To a certain extent frozen food loses some nutritional value, but is far more beneficial than cooked/processed food.

Summarized List Of Raw Barf Diet Foods

» Raw meaty bones and muscle meat from: chicken, pork, beef, rabbit and lamb

» Offal/organ meats: liver, kidney, heart etc

» Eggs

» Dairy produce: milk, butter, cheese, yoghurt.

» Seafood: All oily fish

» Vegetables: Dark green leaves, mushrooms, brassicas, root veg, salad veg etc.

» Fruits: Most fruits but definitely not grapes and the dried varieties such as raisens, sultanas etc

» In addition brewers yeast as an excellent source of the B complex vitamins.

» The polyunsaturated oils mentioned.

Food Separation And Combination

Food combination and separation relates to the idea that food should be neither cooked nor combined in one complete diet. The premise of the commercially processed food is that the 'complete balanced' diet is cooked and contains a combination of food groups that the dog receives at each and every meal.

Ian Billinghurst suggests that wild dogs, feral dogs or whatever, will never eat a balanced meal (in other words, all of the food groups represented in one meal) and that a balanced diet is reached over time. So he suggests that one meal is likely to consist of entirely vegetarian in the form of the stomach contents or guts of a herbivore killed (This is usually the first thing a carnivore will eat, particularly if it is starving and needs to be nourished quickly). Another meal will be offal; liver, kidney, heart etc. Another will be muscle. Another, predominantly fat. Yet another will be entirely bones, which may well be one of the final parts of the animal eaten as all the rest is picked and stripped over a number of days.

So if the dog took this approach, day one would consist of all of the vitamins, minerals, carbohydrates and fibre mentioned as part of the vegetation food group. Day two is likely to be partly protein, but also the vitamins and other elements associated with liver and the other offal meats. Day three would be mostly protein. Day four would be mostly essential fatty acids via the fat. Day five would be mostly the minerals of the bones. So in this hypothetical scenario over a 5 day cycle the dog has received protein on mainly one day, vegetation on mainly one day, essential fatty acid on only one day. To be fair, vitamins, minerals and other elements will be present on each day, but not in the concentrations assumed for protein or carbohydrates or essential fatty acids.

Food combining is particularly problematic where calcium is concerned. As previously noted, calcium causes all sorts of problems with the absorption of essential minerals such as zinc, copper and iron. So it would be best to feed a product that has very little calcium but a good source of zinc, copper, iron and other minerals, separately from a relatively high calcium intake. Feeding offal, such as liver, kidneys, heart etc, allows your dog to feed in this way, similar to the way it would feed on a wild kill. It generally would have its daily feed of offal, and as offal is digested relatively quickly this should mean that any bone/calcium absorption should not interfere with the mineral absorption.

The advantage with a food separation diet is that certain raw foods that may seem high in certain elements are really not being given on a constant every day basis. One of the big problems with processed foods are that a lot of the same elements such as calcium and phosphorus, protein and salt, are given daily. The result of that is an overload of those nutrients and all of the consequential problems on various organs of the body, such as overworked kidneys, liver etc.

A lot of the food separation practice involves keeping proteins and starch foods separate and therefore promoting greater health.

Raw meaty bones should be fed separately from other elements such as the vegetables. The key to a healthy balanced diet is not the way dogs are fed on a commercially processed diet. In this case, they receive every element, i.e. protein, carbohydrate, fats, vitamins, minerals etc all in one go, and on each day. This causes a lot of problems in the natural functioning of the dogs body. The correct, natural way should be to make each meal different and separate the different elements to ensure no overload takes place and no mixing of certain elements likely to conflict with each other.

Balanced diet in this case is your dogs natural eating habits take place, and not the artificially forced balance of commercially processed foods. In a sense, we are bound to eat different meals each day, but they are bound to be a combination of protein, carbohydrate and fat, with the associated vitamins and minerals of those foods. Dogs are not designed to eat that way.

Feeding Dogs Bones

There seems to be a common misconception that feeding bones to dogs is dangerous. There are obviously many horror stories of bones splintering and causing internal bleeding, bones having to be surgically removed, impacted bones in the gut, dogs having bones hanging out of their rear end as they try to pass them, etc. Most of these problems however, happen with cooked bones. Bones that are cooked effectively dry out and lose their relative elasticity and become hard, brittle and splinter prone.

Raw Bones

Raw bones, despite their hard, solid form are still living tissue full of nutrients. As well as marrow, essential fat, anti oxidant properties and enzymes, they also contain calcium and phosphorus in a perfect balance, necessary for a dogs needs. As previously noted the raw meaty bone/BARF diet is also suitable for growing puppies as well as older dogs. In fact many owners and breeders insists this is their preferred way of raising puppies. This is particularly the case when we consider that puppies require sufficient phosphorus and calcium whilst growing and raw meaty bones take away the guess work of how much calcium and phosphorus you would otherwise have to feed if feeding processed food. Again, Ian Billinghurst states that bones actually contain the exact proportions of calcium and phosphorus needed. Again this has been a problem where some breeders over supplement calcium, when feeding a commercial diet.

Raw meaty bones also provide all of the essential amino acids your dog needs.

Incidentally, from the point of view of essential fatty acids, pork and chicken bones are a richer source than beef and lamb, which have relatively low amounts. That isn't to say that you should not feed beef and lamb bones also. They do have the same mineral and protein value, but lack the same high level of essential fatty acids that pork and chicken have.

Raw bones are also excellent sources of the fat soluble vitamins A, D and E. When bones are cooked, those vitamins are lost, which is another important reason why you should never feed dogs cooked bones. Cooking bones also destroys much of the nutrients of the bone marrow. Similarly to the A, D and E vitamins, the marrow is an excellent source of nutrients vital for a strong immune system. This not only fights infection and generally keeps our dogs in peak health, but also promotes longevity.

As well as the meat component, the bone in combination is said to provide the dog with its entire protein requirements. However, caution must be exercised where a dog has become obese. Please bear in mind that feeding raw meaty bones is an important addition for any dog. But because of the highly nutritious energy giving properties of raw meaty bones, giving too many will only add to the obesity. But again, please do include a moderate amount regularly as part of their diet.

It is suggested by advocates of raw meaty bones feeding that they will in themselves provide just about every nutrient your dog will need. The benefits include:

» All of the important minerals

» Essential fatty acids

» Vitamins A, D and E (as previously noted, the K vitamin is manufactured in the bowel of the dog)

» Enzymes

» Antioxidants

» Optimum protein needs

» Most of the B vitamins (as well as vitamin C to an extent, dogs produce their own B complex vitamins)

» Blood forming and immunity benefits of marrow

A raw meaty bone diet is suitable for every dog whether Rottweiler or Pug. It is also suitable for every age group. In essence it is suitable for lactating female dogs, working dogs, growing pups, senior dogs, as long as their teeth are sound.

Buried Bones

Raw buried bones will gradually decompose with their own natural enzymes, and should be perfectly healthy for dogs to eat. The cooking process of bones however, kills the enzymes and although they still decompose, it is bacteria that is involved, which in turn can produce toxins that could make your dog seriously ill. Incidentally, the likely reason your dog is burying bones is over feeding. So their natural survival instinct takes over, and any left over is saved for later.

Teeth Cleaning

If dogs are not given the opportunity to chew, rip and crush bones, such as when they are fed soft processed food, their teeth and gums will suffer. The very action of chewing on meat and bones generally cleans the teeth, scrapes away tarter, massages the gums and teeth. The obvious advantages of this are a lack of gum disease, tooth decay, abscesses and a decreased chance of the body being poisoned via an infected mouth. In addition, the breath of bone chewing dogs rarely smells.

Problems Feeding Mostly Organ Meat

Constant feeding of heart, kidney, steak, tongue, liver etc, have been known in the long term to produce an imbalance and consequent disease. One such case involved the dog developing hepatitis which manifested in lethargy, arthritis, skin disease as well as high cholesterol. This type of diet produced an overload of protein, phosphorus, Vitamin A and a deficiency of calcium.

Problems Feeding Mostly Fish

Certain raw fish contains an enzyme that destroys B1 vitamins. Oily fish fats affect Vitamin E. This is usually more significant if fillets of fish are given and not whole fish. The dog would benefit from eating the bones, head, internal organs that are all likely to contain the necessary B and E vitamins. Once again, feeding fish occasionally is perfectly acceptable, but as a main dietary source will cause all manner of complications.

Problems Feeding Mostly Meat

A dogs diet consisting of mostly meat and in particular cooked meat, can result in diseases associated with skin diseases such as eczema, heart and kidney disease, arthritis and at worse cancer.

Similarly as above with an all offal diet, a meat only diet, is significantly lacking in calcium to the extent that they would only be receiving about 5% of their actual requirements. As you may well expect, the main problem with all meat is the concentration of protein. In addition, phosphorus levels are excessive. There would also be notable deficiencies of Vitamins A, D and E together with copper and iodine. The lack of calcium as well as the other vitamins and minerals deficiencies, in particular would also be extremely detrimental to a growing puppy. Even if these were supplemented in some way, it is never advisable and there are much better, safer ways of feeding them. But again, as with the other specific food only diets, in moderation meat is an essential component of a balanced diet.

e) Types of Commercial Dog Food

There are three main types of commercial dog food; wet, dry, and semi-moist. Dry dog foods are the most commonly used and they are also referred to as "kibble". This type of food is typically packed in a bag and they are usually extruded in the form of pellets. Dry dog foods come in a wide variety of flavors and formulas and they have a fairly low moisture content. Wet dog food obviously has a higher moisture content. They are typically cooked at very high temperatures to sterilize them and then packaged in pressure-sealed containers. Semi-moist dog foods come in the form of soft, chewy pellets typically packaged in pouches or sachets.

In addition to these types of commercial dog food there are a few other options. Dehydrated dog food is becoming popular among pet owners who want to feed their dog's fresh or raw food but who want a product with a longer shelf life. Fresh dog food comes in refrigerated or frozen varieties and it is one of the most expensive options when it comes to commercial dog food. Fresh dog food can also be freeze-dried to remove most of the moisture content (thereby increasing the shelf life) without resulting in a loss of nutrients by cooking.

The type of dog food you choose for your Bichon Frisé is largely a matter of preference. Most dog owners choose dry food because it is the most cost-effective option and because it lasts the longest. If your dog has food allergies or special dietary restrictions, a fresh or frozen dog food may be a better option because these foods are often made with limited ingredients. Senior dogs, who have trouble chewing dry food may prefer moist or semi-moist foods. You can also just soak dry food in water or broth to soften it.

Problems With Dry Food

» Dried processed formulas are the cheapest and most convenient to use but are generally the worst of all the processed dog foods.

» Processed food, particularly dried 'kibble' has in some cases been found to contain an insufficient amount of zinc

» Generally made up of ground cooked bone and offal with cereal

» They have a low nutritional value and are hard to digest.

» Contain excess calcium and starch

» These large amounts of calcium can cause bloat and bone problems. Calcium is also responsible for zinc deficiency, because when calcium combines with zinc it results in a mixture that cannot be absorbed.

» Zinc is an essential ingredient and a lack of it can result in problems associated with growth, skin, infertility, pancreatitis, diabetes etc.

- Low in vitamins, minerals, protein, essential fatty acids and promotes tarter build up

- Lack of essential fatty acids contributes to skin diseases and problems associated with growth and reproduction

As most dry feed contains insufficient amounts of essential fatty acids this to large extent is a major contributory factor to severe skin conditions. The conventional drugs and medical treatments used to treat these conditions, generate massive revenues to the veterinary medical industry year in year out. Money wasted by you the consumer not to mention the discomfort and suffering to the dog.

- Fats and vitamins that are present, quickly deteriorate resulting in an even lower nutritional value after only a few weeks.

- Low in energy value and high in insoluble fibre

- Can cause bladder infections and stones which can result in difficulty passing urine and may require surgery or special diets to remove the obstruction

Problems With Semi Moist Food

This is considered to be marginally better than dry dog food. The energy levels are higher due to an increased carbohydrate content derived from ingredients such as corn syrup

They contain a low water content, about 30% and certain additives/preservatives to give them a greater shelf life.

As they have a similar composition to dry food, they are also associated with much the same diseases and other health issues.

Problems With Canned Food.

There is a very high water content present in canned food, approximately 80%. So in other words, what nutritional value that remains makes up only 20% of what you are buying.

The cost of buying tinned dog food in comparison to dry food is usually at least double. Again the ingredients are similar to the other processed foods, but in general the percentage of cereal is less and animal derivatives, more.

They are also in general more palatable to dogs than the others probably due to the moist meaty texture.

As with all canned products, their two main advantages are a greater shelf life and are extremely convenient. Other than that, they carry the same health problems as the other types of processed foods.

Problems With Tarter Build Up

Where dogs are given the opportunity to rip, tear and crunch raw meaty bones their teeth are cleaned and gums massaged. With processed foods this function is lost. Even dry food where it is thought that the dry composition has an abrasive, cleaning effect. The result of chewing raw meaty bones, is that their mouth generally remains healthy and odour free. Contrast this with dogs fed on processed food and we take it for granted that the rancid 'dogs breath' is normal.

The high levels of carbohydrate and calcium in processed foods are thought to be a major contributing factor to tarter build up that attacks the teeth and gums. Eventually this leads to serious gum disease and tooth decay. Tartar harbours bacteria, which in turn feed off and thrives on the carbohydrates present in processed food. These bacteria attack and infect the mouth in general and specifically the teeth and gums causing painful gum infections and tooth decay, resulting in rancid breath and ultimately tooth loss.

In 1993 it was reported that 90% of dogs in the U.S.A ate processed dog food. In addition, veterinary dental treatment was said to represent over one third of vets income. In 2014 according to some surveys, processed dog food consumption was thought to be around 85%

Not only does this mouth bacteria cause serious localized problems, but the bacteria has a general toxic effect on the whole body, causing general ill health. The bacteria enters the blood stream and seriously affects the major organs of the body causing diseases of the lungs, heart, kidneys and reproductive organs etc.

As the legal obligation of manufacturers is that their 'complete formulas', contain a minimum level of certain nutrients, it is fair to assume that there isn't necessarily a specified amount. Some scientific analysis carried out in Australia showed certain foods contained less vitamins than the legal requirement. In some cases there was an excess. Obviously if your dog requires a certain level of nutrients for optimum health, if this is lacking they will develop diseases associated with a deficiency. In a similar way, an overload of certain vitamins or minerals can cause diseases and health problems. Excess protein for example can cause kidney disease. Excess sodium is associated with heart disease. As you know excess calcium causes zinc deficiency as well as growth problems and bloat. Over time, this can result in the devastating effect of major organ failure.

Why Is The Complete/ Balanced Diet, That The Commercial Package Promotes, Such A Problem.

The idea of having a complete balanced diet in one convenient package sounds like a great idea. The problem is, as we have already discovered, if certain elements such as calcium are allowed to interact with other essential minerals such as zinc and copper, they result in indigestibility of those minerals. The complete diet which effectively combines a whole host of nutrients means that if it is the only source of zinc or copper etc, then the body will likely not be absorbing those elements which results in a deficiency. The same problem occurs when B complex vitamins go through the heat process of cooking and also interact with other certain elements. They too can become immobilized and not ingested.

So the problem arises when we attempt to feed the dog all of the elements combined. Once again, by combining certain elements, they interact and interfere with their individual effectiveness. In its wild primitive state, the dog would be unlikely to ever get a chance to have all of those elements together in one meal.

There are similar problems when mixing protein and starch. Early scientific research into digestion feed trials for dogs, largely involved the separate feeding of starch rich foods and protein. Significant results were noted that dramatically altered the health of patients.

f) Reading the Ingredients List

Again, legal requirements state that food contains minimum recommended amounts of certain nutrients. Labelling does not necessarily have to state that the food will be the best option in terms of your dogs health, longevity, reproduction, growth. There will certainly be no mention that the food will probably lead to a premature death and a number of associated health issues.

Some of the reasons manufacturers process dog food the way they do include: greater shelf life and the ability to take questionable ingredients and make a product more appealing to the consumer, namely us the public.

As previously mentioned, in order to create this greater shelf life, most of the nutrients or everything that would otherwise benefit the dog, such as enzymes and micro organisms, have to be removed. The most efficient way of doing this is by cooking. Preservatives such as salt and sugar will be added which in addition to promoting a greater shelf life, also make them more appetising to the dog.

Having said that, as previously noted,commercially produced dog food seems to be the most popular option for dog owners. Like many other dog owners, you have the choice to feed your dog this way if you wish. As with most products, some are better than others. If you do opt for processed dog foods, whether as a temporary measure or otherwise,please do take the time to evaluate different brands and formulas. The best way to do this is by looking at the label and the ingredients list. For customers in the U.S.A, when you evaluate a bag of dog food for instance, the first thing you should look for is a statement of nutritional adequacy from the American Association of Feed Control Officials (AAFCO). The statement should look something like this:

"[Product Name] is formulated to meet the nutritional levels established by the AAFCO Dog Food nutrient profiles for [Life Stage]."

The American Association of Feed Control Officials is responsible for monitoring and regulating what goes into animal feed including pet foods. This organization has set standards that pet foods must meet in order to be considered nutritionally adequate for dogs in certain life stages; puppy, adult, and senior. If the dog food label does not carry an AAFCO statement of nutritional adequacy, you should move on to another option. On the other hand, just because a product carries the AAFCO statement doesn't necessarily mean that it is good for your dog.

In the United Kingdom, the Pet Food Manufacturer's Association (PFMA) exists to provide pet owners with guidance for selecting pet foods. This organization is the principal trade body for the U.K. pet food industry with more than 70 member companies, representing about 90% of the U.K. pet food market. The PFMA does not put a statement on pet food labels in the same way as AAFCO; but they do strive to raise pet food industry standards and to promote pet food products deemed as safe and nutritious.

However, there is also a new fact sheet on labeling with regards to the pet food ingredients list. As a Bichon Frisé dog owner you should always be checking and improving your dogs health, wellbeing, weight and shape. PFMA has a downloadable Dog Size-O-Meter that you can keep on hand. For more information, visit:

pfma.org.uk/dog-pet-size-o-meter/

Everything that we eat contributes to our health. The same will apply to your Bichon Frisé. He is entirely dependent on what you feed him. Keep in mind that although you may be thinking that your Bichon Frisé looks healthy enough, it takes years for a not so healthy dog food to take its toll on your Bichon Frisé's health.

For more information about pet food labelling standards in the U.K., visit the PFMA website here:

http://www.pfma.org.uk/labelling

The European Pet Food Industry Federation

This federation was formed in 1970 and represents the pet food industry in 26 countries. This representation is carried out via their network of 18 national or regional pet food industry associations. The main goal of this federation is to promote the views and interests of around 650 European pet food producing companies. Its goal is to make sure that all pet food manufactured is safe, nutritious and palatable. For more information, visit:

http://www.fediaf.org/who-we-are/

The U.S. Food and Drug Administration (FDA)

The FDA releases press releases regarding pet food recalls from the firms involved. The FDA is an organization that consists of the Office of the Commissioner and four directorates overseeing core functions of the agency. To learn more, visit:

http://www.fda.gov also http://www.foodsafety.gov/

The best way to truly evaluate the nutritional value of a pet food is to examine the ingredients list. Dog food labels include a complete list of ingredients that is organized in descending order by volume. This means that the ingredients present in the highest quantity/volume appear at the beginning of the list. This makes it easy for you to get a quick sense of a product's nutritional value. If the first few ingredients are healthy ingredients, the product is probably a good choice. If however, the first few ingredients are low-quality fillers, you should move on.

When evaluating the ingredients list for a commercial dog food, you want to see a high-quality source of protein listed first. Fresh meats like chicken, turkey, beef, and fish are good options but do not be turned off if you see something like chicken meal. Fresh meats contain about 80% water so, once the dog food is cooked, their weight is much less than the original. Meat meals have already been cooked down to a moisture content around 10% so they contain up to 300% more protein than fresh meats. A high-quality commercial dog food might list a fresh meat first followed by a meat meal second.

In addition to high-quality protein sources, you should also look for digestible carbohydrates and animal-based fats in the ingredients list. Carbohydrates that are easily digestible for dogs include things like cooked brown rice, oats, and barley. Be wary of wheat and corn-based products however, because these ingredients often trigger food allergies in dogs and they are low in nutritional value. The number of carbohydrate sources on the ingredients list is also important to consider. Dogs do not require a great deal of carbohydrate. Only about 15% of your dog's diet should come from carbohydrates. Low-quality dog foods contain as much as 30% to 70% of this nutrient.

If you see an ingredient like chicken fat or poultry fat on the label for a commercial pet food, do not be turned off as it is a good thing! As you learned previously, fats are a highly concentrated form of energy and they play an important role in your dog's diet. Fats from animal-based sources are particularly beneficial so you should look for things like chicken fat and fish oil in your dog's food. Plant-based fats like flaxseed oil and canola oil can also be beneficial but animal-based fats are more biologically valuable to your dog.

In addition to the main ingredients on a dog food label you also need to pay attention to the things near the end of the list. This is where pet food manufacturers like to sneak in things like artificial flavors, colorants, and preservatives. Avoid ingredients with the word "by-product" attached, as well as chemical preservatives like BHA and BHT. Be aware that these ingredients might be spelt out instead of abbreviated. You should also avoid things like corn syrup, MSG, food dyes, and low-quality filler ingredients like corn and wheat gluten.

So when you next look at a dog food label,as well as the ingredients, consider the following:

Does a food label or advertising assert that the food has been tested on dogs over a long term, and therefore state that the product supports long term health, a long life, effective for reproduction and growth? If not then you need to question why not? If they could state these long term health benefits then they would certainly be advertising the facts.

So in short:

» Will the food keep the dog healthy?

» Will the food fulfil the needs of growing puppies?

» Will the food aid dental health, produce healthy litters of puppies, ensure adult dogs remain healthy and live to a ripe old age?

In essence, is there proof via scientific data, that the food has been proven to promote health, longevity, dental health, delayed aging and absence of degenerative diseases. Obviously in order to prove that, clinical trials will need to have been carried out over a dogs lifetime. In other words, the claims made by manufacturers is not based on speculative assumptions. It would also need to be proved that the dog is in excellent health and this is due to being fed on this particular diet. The type of proof needs to demonstrate that trials were carried out by an unbiased independent laboratory. You would also need to see the actual food analysis found.

g) Bichon Frisé Feeding – What's in the Tin

The quality of commercially prepared dog food is a hot topic. The dog food industry is a high earning one and often owned by huge corporations that often put profit before the health of our dogs. Many dog food ingredients are not fit for human consumption and although vitamins are added to dog foods we cannot be certain whether they are of good enough quality to have an effect on the health of our dogs. Unless an ingredients list on a bag or tin of dog food is completely transparent the meat within dog food is usually rendered and described as 'meal' or 'derivatives'.

But what do these hazy terms actually mean

Rendering is a process which involves putting bones, carcasses, beaks, hooves and tails into a huge tub and heating it so high that any virus cells, bacteria or antibiotic content dies. The fat content rises to the top and is scooped away. The remnants are ground up into a hot pink sludge of body parts. And this substance is what will eventually become commercial dog food. Does it sound terrifying? It does, that's because it is. Rendered foods are permanently deemed unfit for human consumption for health reasons. Yet we unknowingly feed it to our dogs. After the food becomes kibble it is colored to look nice and then sprayed with fat, in order to tempt dogs to eat it. Tinned foods have a lot of salt added, as do the little pouches meant for small dogs, which is no good for the dog's heart.

Thankfully and due to many different investigations inclusive of the dog food project by Sabine Contreras many smaller business are developing better food, made from whole food ingredients that are much better for our dogs. www.dogfoodproject.com describes the entire investigation and is well worth a read.

Admittedly the following article relates to 2007, but it still makes scary reading as to how the so called safe dog food diets can infiltrate the food chain with contaminated supplies.

https://en.wikipedia.org/wiki/2007_pet_food_recalls

Again, negative feedback about BARF diets, such as the threat of Salmonella and Listeria monocytogenes strains, has been predominantly asserted by the FDA. In 2011 as part of a study between 2010 and 2012, by the FDA Center for Veterinary Medicine, 196 samples of raw dog food were analysed. This was in the form of frozen ground meat. 15 proved positive for Salmonella and 32 for Listeria monocytogenes. Again it is not fair to comment whether or not this sample represents a fair overall reflection of contamination threat in all cases. Or whether those figures would be the same with a different set of samples. My own personal experience of feeding raw meaty bones is that my supplier is a wholesale pork butcher and I receive this in 25kg bags approx which I then portion up and freeze. I also purchase frozen supermarket chicken portions. I feed 1 portion of chicken thigh per dog per day, and in both cases the meat is served whole and not ground. I have never had any problem with either a sick dog or the suggested issues with feeding bones.

Once again, the dog owners who favor raw feeding and oppose processed foods, believe the contamination risks suggested by FDA outweigh the obvious benefits gained to the dogs health. Although the FDA do not recommend raw diets they do acknowledge that there are pet owners prefer to feed this way and furthermore suggest ways to deal with these possible contaminants

You can read the full article here:

http://www.fda.gov/AnimalVeterinary/ResourcesforYou/AnimalHealthLiteracy/ucm373757.htm

For additional information on processed dog food, please read the following:

http://www.dailymail.co.uk/news/article-2546512/How-pet-food-killing-dog-feeding-parsnips-yoghurt.html

h) Quality Commercial Foods for Bichon Frisés

Once again, if you are considering trying commercial dog foods, you will find included here several brands to look at as examples of what you might consider quality dog food. The commercial dog foods available in your area might differ according to the pet store chains available as well as the distribution policies for certain brands. The commercial dog foods available in your area might differ according to the pet store chains available as well as the distribution policies for certain brands. Below you will find a list of several commercial dog food formulas that are recommended for small breeds like the Bichon Frisé:

Earthborn Holistic Small Breed Formula

This holistic dog food formula is specially designed to meet the nutritional and energy needs of small-breed dogs like the Bichon Frisé. Earthborn Holistic Small Breed dry food is made with high-quality sources of animal-based protein like chicken meal and whitefish meal to make sure your dog maintains healthy lean body mass while also providing for his energy requirements. This formula is rich in antioxidants, dietary fiber, amino acids, and fatty acids to ensure well-balanced nutrition. Earthborn Holistic Small Breed dry food also provides a balance of omega-3 and omega-6 fatty acids to support healthy skin and coat which is especially important for the Bichon Frisé.

Nutro Natural Choice Small Breed Dog Food

This Natural Choice small breed dog food from Nutro is designed with a special balance of proteins and fats to meet the high energy needs of small-breed dogs. This formula is made with fresh chicken and chicken meal as the top two ingredients. There are also several whole grains such as brown rice and oatmeal, as well as chicken fat for concentrated energy. This Natural Choice small breed dog food is loaded with antioxidants to support your dog's immune system as well as a balance of omega-3 and omega-6 fatty acids for healthy skin and coat.

Blue Buffalo Life Protection Formula for Small Breed

This Life Protection Formula for small-breed dogs from Blue Buffalo is designed to meet the high energy needs of small-breed dogs. This formula is made with top-quality proteins like de-boned chicken as well as wholesome whole grains, fruits, and vegetables. This Life Protection Formula from Blue Buffalo is free from corn, wheat, and soy as well as artificial flavors, preservatives, and colors. Additionally, this formula is enhanced with a precise blend of antioxidants, vitamins and minerals as well as fatty acids for concentrated energy and healthy skin and coat.

Wellness Small Breed Complete Health Adult Formula

This turkey and oatmeal recipe from Wellness is specially designed for small-breed dogs. It is made with four animal-based protein sources to promote lean muscle mass and optimal calorie intake to support healthy body weight. This Wellness Small Breed Complete Health dog food contains a mix of omega-3 and omega-6 fatty acids as well as antioxidants, vitamins, and minerals. This food comes in small pieces which are ideal for small-breed dogs like the Bichon Frisé. It also contains dried fermentation products to support healthy digestion.

Again, I cannot say that any processed feeding regardless of so called quality would be a first choice or preference for me. However, my intention is not to dictate my opinion, but to give an overall picture of what is available. You are then free to make your own mind up and choose. My preference is to feed as natural and healthy as possible, a good quality BARF diet will provide this. Perhaps feeding occasional table scraps or commercial feed when you are pushed for time.

i) How Much to Feed Your Bichon Frisé

Apart from keeping our dogs fit and healthy by feeding its body vital vitamins, minerals and other nutrients, the main thing that food provides is energy. This energy is obtained from all the main food groups including carbohydrates, protein and fats. Again, they need to be given in the correct amounts for the dogs needs. Not enough of those elements would result in malnutrition, too many would naturally lead to obesity. It is all about when a dog most needs these food elements. This will be most needed for purposes of reproduction and puppy growth. Times of stress and extreme activity levels such as may be expected from working sled or farm dogs. Cold weather will also see a need for extra food resources. Strangely enough the opposite is not the case. Whilst we live on light meals such as salad during hot spells, dogs use a considerable amount of energy in order to cool down, by panting.

Where a dogs diet needs to account for these extreme uses of energy, it is necessary to bear in mind the energy values of the three major food groups. Weight for weight, fat is by far the richest of the three in terms of energy value, in fact this is actually double either carbohydrate or protein. If the dog needs an energy rich diet because it is a working dog, for example, then a fat rich diet would be appropriate. This type of feeding for a dog that is not burning the fat off, would result in an obese dog destined for health problems. In general, you should be very careful not to over feed your dog. Obviously the opposite of this is also true, you do not want to underfeed your dog, because being under weight is also unhealthy for your dog. It is not an easy remedy to keep your dog at an optimum weight. You can usually see if the dog is over or under weight. A more accurate way is to weigh the dog on a regular basis and feed accordingly. Again, I would personally take the ideal weight for your type of dog as a guideline and then as accurately as you possibly can, provide meals that will keep your dog at an ideal weight. And once again, routinely weigh the dog to see where any fluctuations occur. You will soon get an idea of whether your dog is getting enough food. Also remember to take into account periods of extra activity as mentioned previously.

As you have already learned, your Bichon Frisé's calorie needs will vary according to his age and activity level. When your Bichon Frisé is a puppy it is sometimes recommended that you allow him to eat as much as he likes. Please do bear in mind, that the type of food I refer to here is dry kibble type dog food, not perishable cooked or raw food that will quickly go off if left unrefrigerated all day. But again, refer back to the previous chapter and remember that he should be eating whatever the breeder has been feeding initially. But also remember that a lean breed such as a Bichon Frisé is highly unlikely to put too much weight on even as an adult. Most dogs are good about eating when they are hungry and stopping when they are full. In this respect, if you were to feed so many meals per day, you may find that your puppy will not eat certain meals. If your puppy isn't obviously ill, it is likely to be that he doesn't need the extra food. So do not worry too much about serving him a precise amount each time. If he leaves some it is fair to assume he is eating all the calories he needs to fuel his growth and development at that meal.

» Generally, you may be told that from 8 weeks to 12 weeks their daily food ration should be split into 4 meals.

» From 12 weeks to 26 weeks this should be reduced to 3 meals per day.

» 26 weeks to 52 weeks, this is further reduced to 2 meals per day.

At one year and after, most dog owners will be feeding either one or two meal per day. I prefer to feed twice per day. Around 10 am I provide almost all of their daily requirement. On some days they eat everything and then perhaps the next day only half. If they eat everything, I do not give any extra now, but feed a second meal around 3pm. This is about half that of the first meal. They get nothing else, no treats etc, until around 10 am the next day. If however they have left some from 10 am, I refrigerate that and they get get along with some extra, perhaps not half as much again. They get fresh clean water all of the time which is changed at least once per day. Again, this is for two adult dogs. You could feed your puppy in the same way, but again with the extra meals included.

The important thing to realize is that you use a good quality puppy food. As to how much you give per meal, if you are splitting the meals, depends on the weight of your pup and the recommended amount stated on your brand of food. Again, a lot depends on the quality and therefore nutritional value of the product, which is why it is important to not skimp on price especially for puppy food.

But whichever plan you follow, once your puppy reaches maturity you should start rationing his meals. You can choose how many meals to give your Bichon Frisé each day, but again most dog owners recommend dividing your dog's daily portion into two meals. To help you determine how much to feed your dog, follow the feeding suggestions on the dog food package in relation to the previous calorie needs mentioned. Keep in mind that feeding suggestions are just that, suggestions, so you may need to make adjustments. Start off with the recommended amount for a few weeks. If your dog gains weight you'll need to cut back a bit. If he loses weight, you should increase his rations a bit. You can always ask your veterinarian for suggestions if you aren't sure whether your dog is at a healthy weight.

Keep in mind that during the puppy stage you'll need to:

- Ensure that your Bichon Frisé puppy is gaining weight steadily by frequent veterinary check ups during the puppy stage. You can also buy a scale and weigh him every week.
- Watch out for obesity
- Feed the correct puppy diet appropriate to instructions given by your vet or the dietary guidelines on the back of the food package you buy your Bichon Frisé.
- Avoid feeding only a one-sided diet of meat only. Mix with other natural food stuff.
- Avoid feeding your puppy poor quality commercial dog food, any junk food or table scraps that contain empty calories
- Keep your Bichon Frisé away from dangerous foods like chocolate, grapes, candy and gum that can be deadly to dogs

Another factor you need to consider in regard to feeding your Bichon Frisé is how many treats you give him. When you are training your puppy, you should use very small treats. Even if your puppy eats a lot of them, however, it will not be a problem because he needs a lot of calories to fuel his growth. Once your Bichon Frisé is fully mature, however, you should limit the number of treats you give him to avoid going over his daily calorie needs.

For Bichon Frisés with ingredient intolerances or food sensitivities, choose a brand with a single-source of animal protein and real deboned meat as the first ingredient and a healthy, simple list of additional grain-free, gluten-free ingredients. Many health problems in Bichon Frisés can be avoided by feeding a high quality grain-free diet. Yet one needs to pay attention to the ingredient list even though it's labeled as grain-free.

j) Summary of Nutritional Information

- Nutritional Needs: water, protein, carbohydrate, fats, vitamins, minerals
- RER: 30 (weight in kg) + 70

- Calorie Needs: varies by age, weight, and activity level; RER modified with activity level
- Amount to Feed (puppy): feed freely but consult recommendations on the package
- Amount to Feed (adult): consult recommendations on the package; calculated by weight
- Important Ingredients: fresh animal protein (chicken, beef, lamb, turkey, eggs), digestible carbohydrates, animal fats
- Important Minerals: calcium, phosphorus, potassium, magnesium, iron, copper and manganese
- Important Vitamins: Vitamin B Complex, Vitamins D, A, E, C, K
- Look For: AAFCO statement of nutritional adequacy; protein at top of ingredients list; no artificial flavors, dyes, preservatives

k) Toxic Foods Affecting Bichon Frisé Dogs

In addition to making sure that you provide your Bichon Frisé with a healthy diet, you also need to be careful NOT to feed him certain foods. It can be tempting to give your dog a few scraps from your plate but certain "people foods" can actually be toxic for your dog.

Below you will find a list of foods that can be harmful to your Bichon Frisé:

- Alcohol
- Apple seeds
- Avocado
- Cherry pits
- Chocolate
- Cocoa mulch fertilizer
- Coffee
- Garlic
- Grapes/raisins
- Gum (can cause blockages and sugar free gums may contain the toxic sweetener Xylitol)
- Hops
- Macadamia nuts
- Mold
- Mushrooms
- Mustard seeds
- Nuts
- Onions and onion powder/leeks

- Peach pits
- Potato leaves/stems
- Rhubarb leaves
- Tea
- Tomato leaves/stems
- Walnuts
- Xylitol
- Yeast dough

If your Bichon Frisé gets into a food that he shouldn't have, you should call the Pet Poison Control Hotline, just to be on the safe side. The specialist on the other end of the line will be able to tell you if the amount your dog ingested is potentially toxic. If it is, they will walk you through the steps to induce vomiting to purge the item from your dog's stomach, or recommend that you take your dog to an emergency vet. You may also be able to speak to a licensed veterinarian on the phone for a fee around $65 (£42.25).

L) Toxic Plants Affecting Bichon Frisé Dogs

Not only do you need to be careful about which foods you keep out of your Bichon Frisé's reach, there are also plants that can be toxic to all dogs. If you have any of the houseplants listed below in your house, make sure you keep them well out of your dog's reach. For toxic outdoor plants, remove them from your property or fence them off for your dog's safety.

A list of toxic plants harmful to dogs can be found below:

- Azalea
- Baneberry
- Bird-of-paradise
- Black locust
- Buckeye
- Buttercup
- Caladium
- Castor bean
- Chock-cherries
- Christmas rose
- Common privet
- Cowslip
- Daffodil
- Day lily
- Delphinium
- Easter lily
- Elderberry
- Elephant's ear
- English Ivy

- Foxglove
- Holly
- Horse-chestnut
- Hyacinth
- Iris
- Jack-in-the-pulpit
- Jimsonweed
- Laurels
- Lily of the valley
- Lupines
- May-apple
- Mistletoe
- Morning glory
- Mustards
- Narcissus
- Nightshade
- Oaks
- Oleander
- Philodendron
- Poinsettia
- Poison hemlock
- Potato
- Rhododendron
- Rhubarb
- Sago palm
- Sorghum
- Wild black cherry
- Wild radish
- Wisteria
- Yew

Chapter Five:

Early Training

Every time I learn something new about the biology of dogs I realize how important puppy learning is. Those early stages not only build the body of your Bichon Frisé dog, but also his mind. Which is exactly why I wanted to share these stages of puppy learning with you now.

1.) Bichon Frisé Toilet Training

Do you remember the old saying 'rub his nose in it' For many years this was how house-training was carried out. Poor dogs. In this area of the book we are going to talk about puppy toilet training the right way.

Housebreaking a Bichon Frisé puppy need not be a difficult task. It is simply a case of teaching your dog, as soon as you can, that outside is where the toileting happens.

Bichon Frisé toilet training for success is a matter of putting everything that you can into that first few days. The more times your puppy gets it right in the beginning the quicker he will learn what you want from him. Bichon Frisés are generally known to be very clean, so hopefully you will have few if any accidents, and toilet training should take no time at all.

a.) What Will You Need

For perfect Bichon Frisé toilet training you won't really need a great deal. Some puppy pads or newspaper, an odor neutralizer and a sharp eye along with a swift movement if you notice your puppy needs to go.

I say an odor neutralizer because a generic cleaning product is not enough. General cleansing fluid does not rid the environment of the smell and the dog will always return to a smell when looking for a toilet area. Odor neutralizers literally take the urine into their own particles then disperse and destroy it.

b.) Good Toilet Training Practice

Get into your mind, the idea that for the next few days, you will be a puppy taxi. This involves ferrying your dog outside at least every hour to two hours. In addition, in the case of accidents, picking your little dog up and relocating him to the right place as he starts to toilet.

Similarly it is a good idea to expect to use puppy pads or newspapers in the beginning.

The idea is that in an ideal world, the puppy will go outside to toilet every time. It is still a good idea to have pads present though just in case you miss an opportunity to get him out. The puppy pads/newspapers, can be phased out later. But remember, your puppy has a tiny bladder at the moment and the puppy pad can help with any unexpected toilet mishaps.

You can gradually move the puppy pad toward the external door as the puppy becomes familiar with how to use them. Eventually when the dog heads for it, you can get him straight out of the back door.

Then in time, you may only need to put puppy pads down overnight until your dog's bladder and bowel matures.

Dog understanding, begins with knowing that a dog of any age will repeat any behavior which is rewarded. Things get a little complicated when you look further into it but generally this is the baseline truth.

In addition, the act of rewarding something also teaches the dog to repeat it enough times for it to become a habit.

Putting this into practice, particularly where toilet training is concerned, is actually quite an easy – three step process as follows;

Step One

» Get the environment ready for toilet training by working out where exactly the puppy will be expected to toilet outdoors and sorting out your puppy pads for indoors.

» Place your puppy pads nearby indoors. Puppy pads can be used as the indoor toilet for now whilst your puppy is learning and through the night. As mentioned before, you can substitute pads for newspaper.

» As a rule of thumb, approximately every hour your puppy may need to toilet. But you should commit yourself to look carefully at your puppy for signs that he may need to go at any point. You may see signs such as the following: he may lick his lips, yawn or glance at you. Or if you notice him wandering about, sniffing or circling, anticipate he may need to toilet. If you notice him about to go, it may also be an idea to say something like 'outside for toilets', or 'outside for a wee wee'. You will hopefully get to the stage where as soon as he hears this, he knows you want him to do his toileting outside and will wait at the door. Most dogs get to the stage where they bark to let you know they want letting out to do their toilet business.

Step Two

» Take your puppy outdoors every hour at least. Take him out after he has eaten, slept, played and had a drink because these are the times he will most likely need to go. Take him and wait with him until your puppy toilets, if he needs to.

» Remember this is a baby in the big wild world and he is probably quite insecure. If you push any puppy outdoors to toilet, then leave him out there alone, you are teaching him something and it's not good toilet training.

- So wait with your puppy until he has indeed done his business or he may just come inside and pee at your feet.

- Taxi your puppy outside or to the pad at this point if he has an accident. If he toilets on the pad of his own accord then praise him, as this is a step closer to toileting outside and a step further away from doing it on the floor in the house. You can also begin to move the pad away gradually towards the external door.

Step Three

- When your puppy 'goes' in the place you want him to, it is vital to reward the behavior. Remember that he won't know what you want from him unless you show/tell him. A carefully rewarded behavior will always be repeated.

- Watch your puppy for accidents. Any signs that he may need to toilet, then scoop him up to take him outside or to the nearest puppy pad. This is where you employ that puppy taxi habit.

- Even if your dog has begun to go in the wrong place quickly and quietly ferry him along to his legitimate toileting area. This way you will be alleviating any confusion that he may have about the location of his toilet area.

- Even if he does a tiny bit in the right area still reward him. It can be difficult to learn this for a puppy, particularly as his brain and bladder are still developing; so be kind and patient.

- Keep your eyes peeled because the more successes at this point, the quicker your Bichon Frisé puppy will become housebroken.

Clearing soiled puppy pads/newspaper.

You will need to clear away any soiled paper/pads on a daily basis. You will then want to replenish the area with fresh pads or paper. An important tip to use in the early stages of toilet training is to leave a piece of the soiled, damp paper. This is particularly important for any initial indoor training. The obvious reason for this relates to scent marking. They will naturally return to the area they can smell as scent marked. If you clear the soiled paper and put fresh unscented paper in its place, the pup may not remember where he last went to toilet, or be able to smell the odor. If you leave a piece of the soiled scented paper, he should instantly recognize this as the place to go. It is important that you that this is only in the very initial stages when you are trying to get the puppy to target the puppy pad. Again, once he is successful at this, the next stage is to move the whole thing outside. But again the scented piece will be useful at that stage. Once he knows were he should toilet, leaving the soiled paper will be unnecessary.

c.) HOUSE-TRAINING YOUR BICHON FRISÉ USING THE CRATE.

You have already learned a little bit about the benefits of crating your puppy but in this section you will receive more detailed information about the crate training method. In order for this method to work, your puppy's crate, needs to be just big enough for him to stand, sit, lie down, and turn around in comfortably. If it is too much larger, your puppy might give in to the temptation, and have a toilet accident. You also need to understand that puppies cannot hold their bladders for more than a few hours until they reach six months old. So do not force your puppy to remain in the crate for longer than he can physically restrain himself. In this respect it is probably best to leave him with his crate door open, over night and simply leave paper down. Of course after about six months he will be able to hold this, and you can perhaps close his crate door. But you may find he doesn't soil the paper anyway, if you simply leave the door open, even as an adult.

Before you actually begin crate training your puppy you need to get your puppy used to the crate. If you skip this step in the process, your puppy may learn to associate the crate with bad things, such as you leaving the house. Instead, you should teach your Bichon Frisé puppy that the crate is a good thing.

To do this you can follow these steps:

1. Take the door off the crate, if possible, or prop it open so that it does not close while your puppy is in it.

2. Bring your puppy over to the crate and talk to him in a soothing voice as he explores it.

3. Toss a few treats in and around the crate to encourage your puppy to go inside of his own free will. If treats don't work, try a favorite toy.

4. Start feeding your puppy his meals in the crate. Ideally you should place his food bowl in the back of the crate so he has to go all the way in to eat.

5. Once your puppy is comfortable eating his meals in the crate, you can start to close the door while he is in it. Open the door again as soon as he is finished eating.

6. Each time you feed your puppy in the crate, leave the door closed a few minutes longer until your puppy remains in the crate for 10

minutes after eating.

7. Once your puppy gets used to this, you can start leaving the room for a few minutes after he has already been in the crate for 5 minutes.

8. Slowly increase the amount of time you spend away from your puppy while he is in the crate. If he starts whining or crying, you may have increased the duration of your absence too quickly.

Once your puppy is able to remain in the crate quietly for 30 minutes you can begin crate training. The process of crate training is really quite simple. Your overall aim is to leave your puppy in the crate overnight and when you leave the house. (Some people find that the Bichon Frisé is so well behaved that crates are not necessary. I would still suggest doing the crate training anyway as it can be a useful tool, even if you find you do not really need to use it.) While you are at home, give him plenty of opportunities to do his business outside. If your puppy never has the opportunity to have an accident inside the house, then crate training will not be a chore. It is possible that during the night, your puppy may need to do his toilet business. In this case I would advise lining the crate with newspaper or puppy pads. Most dogs I have known will bark, asking to go out. If it is possible, please do attend to the dog as it will be uncomfortable for him to be expected to hold this until the morning. If you prefer not to keep your dog in his crate overnight then leave him somewhere such as a kitchen with a tiled floor and again plenty of newspaper/puppy pads that can easily be cleaned up.

Providing your puppy is comfortable staying in the crate for extended periods then he should be happy to stay in the crate overnight. You should also be able to extend this to when you are away from home so he doesn't have an accident. Hopefully at this point, he will know exactly what is expected, and be able to refrain from needing to go until the morning. However, if you are woken in the early hours, with his short, "asking to go out", bark, he may need letting outside. Again please don't ignore this, as it will likely be uncomfortable for him to have to hold it until the morning.

For the first few weeks you will need to let your puppy out every few hours until he is old enough to hold his bladder overnight. If you work a full-time job you may need to ask a friend to stop by or hire a dog sitter.

Let your puppy outside immediately after releasing him from the crate, and always give him a chance to go before you put him in it.

If you follow these simple steps you will find that house-training your Bichon Frisé puppy is really quite easy. In many cases, house-training only takes a few weeks. The key is to be as consistent as possible in letting your puppy outside as frequently as you can and in rewarding your puppy for doing his business outside. Your puppy has a natural desire to please you, so praising him for doing his business outside will teach him that you like that behavior and he will be eager to repeat it.

D.) No Punishment

If your puppy has an accident then you were either not watching him carefully enough or you have not taken him out enough. NEVER punish accidents. Simply clean up, and tell yourself that you will do better next time.

Punishment of accidents will cause anxiety around toileting for your puppy and this will simply lead to more accidents. Punishment may even lead to the puppy feeling he needs to eat his own poop. That's not a fair way to raise a puppy.

Older dogs can have housebreaking problems based on a few different things. If a dog has never lived indoors or been house-trained, then he may toilet indoors. This is not his fault as he hasn't been taught the social etiquettes that we live by. You should therefore apply the steps above in the same way to show the dog what you want.

When you bring a rescued Bichon Frisé home, it's important to expect at least a couple of accidents, because he or she will be confused and nervous.

E.) Scent Marking

Male dogs may scent mark in the new home if they are un-neutered or particularly nervous.

Scent marking is the dog's way of showing other dogs that he is there, and can be a nervous reaction or a hormonal response.

Castration can help with the male dog that scent marks, but is not a definite solution as it can cause further insecurity in some worried dogs. It is worth speaking to your vet if you are having a problem like this.

F.) Elderly Dogs

Dogs can lose control of their bladder with old age. This is a sad situation and one which we have to adapt to because we love our dogs. The vet can prescribe specific treatments for leaking and may need to check out your dog's overall health, if this is an issue.

Many dogs fail to make it through the night in the last months/years without needing to go out. Again, the best solution is to put down plenty of newspaper for him to go on. Cleaning this up in the morning is a small sacrifice to pay, as you need to make things as easy and comfortable for them as possible.

2) Why Socialize

Socialization is a complete topic in itself. There are so many dogs in rescue shelters and homes that simply do not know how to react in social situations.

This is because they have never learned what to do in the company of other dogs, children and crowded areas or around other animals.

Stop for a moment and think of street dogs in Europe and similar places. You never see them fighting do you? They manage to get on with no tension and certainly no aggression. They never bark at cars or people.

The street dogs never seem to worry too much about their surroundings. Which points to the fact that there must be a specific reason for the behavior. You guessed it, the reason for poorly socialized dogs is us humans.

We leash them up, stop them interacting, panic when another dog comes towards them and often keep them well away from social situations altogether. Then when a puppy gets to a few months old we complain about their social behavior.

As mentioned previously, it is possible to grasp back some social skills with an older dog, after the socialization boat has sailed. Yet the dog that isn't positively socialized as a puppy, will never really be completely relaxed in new circumstances.

Positive socialization should incorporate everything that you possibly can into a dog's everyday life as early as possible. Not only that though, every experience should be positive.

A good socialization schedule will include positive experiences of and with;

» As many dogs as possible

» Buses

» Cars

» Children

» Domestic animals

» Farmed animals

» People of all ages

» Push chairs

» Sounds such as recorded thunder and fireworks

» The groomer (if you are to use a professional)

» Trains or trams

» Unusual looking people (those wearing hats and unusual clothing)

» The veterinary surgery

» Wildlife

Your dog will need to learn canine manners from other dogs. He is socialized with exposure to the aforementioned list, to build his personal confidence and ability to cope in new situations as he grows.

Although Bichon Frisés are known to be relatively placid, sensitive dogs, lack of social skills may easily become borderline aggressive behavior because of a dogs genetic need to defend himself.

So introduce him to as many social situations as possible. He can then learn that most situations are nothing to be afraid of. When you do encounter any of the above, as with any training, always give him lots of praise and show him how pleasant these encounters can be.

3) Other training considerations

a.)Avoid Over Attachment

When your puppy is feeling secure, it is vital to teach him that alone time is normal, even if your lifestyle dictates that the dog will never be left alone, because this prepares your dog for life. Remember the Bichon Frisé can live to a ripe old age, so who knows what the future holds.

Later on we will talk about separation anxiety and how it develops. Yet if you start leaving your puppy early in his life you can certainly minimize the risk. So set up times where you leave him for a short time and try not to allow your puppy to trail around the house after you, following you into every room. This will be particularly important for some Bichon Frisés as they are known to be clingy.

The idea is not to allow your puppy to develop over attachment to you. When a dog becomes over attached they cannot cope with being left alone, simply because you are not there.

Practice leaving your dog with a stuffed Kong, the radio or television on and pop out for a few minutes every day after the first few days.

Make this a priority and part of your dog's learning program because by doing this you minimize the risk of your Bichon Frisé puppy developing distressing separation anxiety later on.

b.) A Nice Relaxed Walk

Bichon Frisés are very adaptable, generally considered to be easy to feed and look after. However, please do not take that to mean that they will be happy to sit at home all day and hardly ever exercise.

Walking Equipment

Dog walking equipment should be introduced carefully, particularly to a puppy, and only the kindest collars or harness types should be used.

The harness is generally better than a collar, as it redistributes the weight of his body and naturally, immediately stops him pulling on the leash.

Dogs are far easier to control on walks when wearing a harness and there is no nasty pulling and coughing, as often happens on a standard collar and leash.

There is never a need to use choke or metal collars on dogs. The same result is easily achievable by using humane equipment and the smallest amount of positive training.

When you first introduce a Bichon Frisé puppy, or older dog, to a collar or harness make it a nice and positive event. Pop it onto the dog and play for a while, then remove it again whilst the dog is still happy.

After doing this a few times, add the leash and allow the dog to trail it behind in the house or garden. Then your puppy should be sufficiently used to it and will be ready to go for a walk.

The following training steps are to help you prevent pulling on the leash. They are simply to make your

Bichon Frisé walking experiences happy and relaxed forever.

The steps may take longer if the dog has learned to grab the leash in his mouth or fight against the tension, but if you persevere they will still work.

Training Steps;

1. With your dog on his leash, walk a couple of steps and if the leash stays slack say the command word ('walk nicely' or something similar. We will talk about the 'heel' command later, so probably the best word would be 'heel') you have chosen for an easy leash and click/reward in quick succession.

2. If the leash is tight you may need to change direction a few times to engineer a slack leash. As soon as any tension vanishes from the leash, carry out the command/click/reward sequence. I sometimes find that by simply stopping, thus breaking the sequence of him pulling, is often enough to make him realize he shouldn't pull. Please don't get into the habit that some 'impatient people' seem to do, and pull the poor dog back with enough force to pull him over. The dog is keen and excited to be out walking and sniffing about. Given the chance he wants to go off and do his own thing. So please be patient and considerate.

Just as an added note here, command/click/reward is referred to previously. If you are not familiar with clicker training, it basically means, as your dog performs a correct action, such as walk nicely you say the command word (so he knows to associate the action with the word). You then use a clicker to mark the behavior (you don't have to use a clicker, you can substitute this with the words 'good boy/girl'). You finally reward the behavior with a treat to begin with, so he associates his action with something good and positive. You will be introduced to more detailed specific training procedures in the next chapter. For now however, simply initiate him walking nicely and as long as he is doing so praise/reward him. I also like to keep repeating the word heel/walk nicely. But make sure he is actually walking nicely so he can associate his act with the word.

Repeat and practice.

Gradually increase the time between when you issue the command, and when you reward. This will keep him keen to carry out the action, as he knows that if he does what you ask, a reward will soon follow. Limiting/delaying the reward also makes it easier when you eventually phase out giving food rewards all together. We will talk about this later.

Again, remember the 'release command' at the end of the session. (If you have come to this part first, without reading about 'release commands', the release is basically as follows: After successfully completing a piece of training, let your dog know they have completed it by releasing them. This can be done in conjunction with the treat stage, and you simply say "finished", "all over", or something similar. Again this is discussed in more detail in a later section.)

Teaching a Bichon Frisé to walk easily on a leash will probably take 3 to 6 training sessions in a quiet area. It will then need practice in various areas, gradually increasing distractions, to become a flawless command. This will require exposure to roads and busy traffic. You will need to get to a point of teaching him to sit and wait at the road side until it is safe to cross.

The time-scale to positive results of this particular lesson depend on how the dog has learned to walk on a leash in his life experiences so far.

Chapter Six:

Training Your Bichon Frisé Dog

In this next chapter we will cover specific step by step obedience training methods for your Bichon Frisé. The Bichon Frisé is a very intelligent breed that typically responds well to training but he can be easily distracted sometimes. For the best success, you should plan to keep your training sessions short and fun so that your Bichon Frisé gets something out of them each time. In addition to receiving step-by-step instructions for training your Bichon Frisé dog, you will also learn the basics about different training methods.

1.) Popular Training Methods

When it comes to training your Bichon Frisé you have a variety of training methods to choose from. Some of the most common training methods include positive reinforcement, punishment-based, alpha dog, and clicker training. In this section you will receive an overview of each training method as well as a recommendation for which option is best for your Bichon Frisé.

a.) Positive-Reinforcement Training

One of the most popular training methods for dogs today is positive reinforcement training. This type of training is a version of operant conditioning in which the dog learns to associate an action with a consequence. In this case, the term consequence does not refer to something bad, it is just something that happens as a result of something else. The goal of positive reinforcement training is to encourage your dog to WANT to do what you want him to do.

The basics of positive reinforcement training are simple, you teach the dog that if he follows your commands he will be rewarded. For example, you teach your dog to respond to the word "Sit" by him sitting down. In order to teach him to associate the command with the action, you reward him with a treat each time he sits on command. It generally only takes a few repetitions for dogs to learn to respond to commands because food rewards are highly motivational for most dogs.

The key to successful positive reinforcement-based training sessions is to keep them short and fun. If the dog enjoys the training, he will be more likely to retain what he has learned. It is also important that you make the connection between the command and the desired response very clear to your dog. If he doesn't understand what you want him to do, he will become confused. It is also important to pair the reward immediately with the desired response. This helps your dog to make the connection more quickly and it motivates him to repeat the desired behavior.

Punishment-Based Training

Punishment-based training is not as harsh as the word suggests. It is not exactly the opposite of positive reinforcement training, but it is very different. While positive reinforcement training is about encouraging your dog to repeat a desired behavior, punishment-based training is about discouraging your dog from performing an unwanted behavior. The goal of punishment-based training is to teach your dog that a certain action results in a negative consequence and thus the dog will choose not to perform that behavior in the future.

The problem with punishment-based training methods is that it is generally only effective in teaching your dog to stop doing something rather than teaching him to respond to a certain command. It is also important to note that punishment-based training can have a negative impact on your relationship with your dog. Even though your dog may stop performing the unwanted behavior, it may not be because you taught him that the behavior is undesirable. He will likely only associate the behavior with fear and pain (depending on the type of punishment you use).

In addition to learning not to perform the behavior in question, your dog will also learn to be fearful of you. If you know anything about dog behavior, you may already know that in most cases, aggression is born of fear. Even the most even-tempered dog can become aggressive if he is afraid. If you use punishment-based training methods you not only risk teaching your dog to fear you, but there is also the possibility that he will become aggressive with you at some point in the future.

Note: I would like to point out here, that if you adopt this style of training, you should NEVER, under any circumstances hit your dog. It is not only cruel, but an unnecessary action on your part. If you are ever having recurring behavioral issues with your dog, you should either seek an alternative approach or in extreme cases, seek the help of a professional dog trainer.

b.) Alpha Dog Training

You may be familiar with this style of training in conjunction with the "Dog Whisperer," Cesar Millan. Cesar Millan is a famous dog trainer who has published a number of books including three New York Times best sellers. Mr Millan's dog training methods are based on the idea that dogs are pack animals and that the dog owner must establish himself as leader of the pack. In doing so, the dog will become submissive and will submit to the owner's will.

According to Cesar Millan's style of training, you should never let your dog walk through a doorway before you and he must wait until you've finished your meal to receive his dinner. Though Mr Millan has a great many followers, there are also many who believe his training methods to be extreme and inhumane. In fact, the RSPCA issued a statement saying that "Adverse training methods which have been seen to be used by Cesar Millan can cause pain and fear for dogs and may worsen their behavioral problems". It is not my intention to discredit Mr Millan or his methods and I cannot personally comment about the effectiveness of his methods. If you are at all interested in this or any other approach, then I urge you to do your own research and make your own mind up. Again, providing you act with kindness, are firm but fair in your dog training approach, then I am sure you will have success which ever method you use.

c.) Clicker Training

Clicker training, as described previously, is a type of positive reinforcement training. With this type of training you use a small clicker device to help your dog form an association with a command and the desired behavior. Because this is the most difficult part of positive reinforcement training, clicker training is often a very quick and effective training method. To use this method you follow the same procedures as you would for positive reinforcement training but you click the clicker as soon as your dog performs the desired behavior and then give him the reward. Once your dog identifies the desired behavior you then stop using the clicker so he does not become dependent on it.

A quick idea of how this works is to firstly get your dog associating the clicker with getting a reward. Usually as soon as the dog hears the clicker he will prick his ears and look towards the clicker or you. When he does, quickly give him the treat, and keep repeating this a few times. You next say the command so if this is sit, say sit and the moment he sits you click and reward. That is basically how this works and how you proceed to other commands.

If you want to get a visual idea of how clicker training works, there are some excellent videos on Youtube, you may wish to check out. Just type clicker training and take your pick. If you are interested in much more detailed information about clicker training, books by Karen Pryor are usually recommended, although I am sure others are useful also.

d. Training Recommendations

It is completely your decision which training method you choose to utilize with your Bichon Frisé but most dog trainers recommend some form of positive reinforcement training. As the Bichon Frisé is considered to be a sensitive gentle personality, you are certainly not recommended to use any harsh treatments. Bichon Frisés are a very intelligent breed so they typically pick things up fairly quickly. Using a clicker may help you to speed up your training sessions as well.

2) Obedience Training – Teaching Basic Commands

By the time you start your puppy with his basic obedience training, he should be about 12 weeks old. By this time he should be very familiar with his toilet training and generally walking about on his lead. While your puppy may not be able to comprehend complex commands right away, you should be able to start basic obedience training at a fairly young age. There are five main commands which form the basics of obedience training; Sit, Down, Come, Stay and Heel. In this section you will receive step-by-step instructions for teaching your Bichon Frisé these five basic commands.

However, before we get started with those basic training commands I want to firstly remind/introduce you to a couple of useful preliminary aspects of his training. In the initial stages of training, please make the training sessions relatively short. Ten or Fifteen minutes of good concentrated practice should be fine initially. When you feel he is keen to carry on, extend these lessons. Or practice these commands frequently at odd times around the house, rather than appoint one session for a designated time. The idea is that you can use the training at a moments notice when required anyway.

a.) The Release Command

If you are coming to this section first, then an explanation is in order. The 'release command' is particularly useful for a number of reasons. It first of all lets your dog know that he has successfully completed a part of his training. It also hopefully lets the dog know the difference between the serious business of sitting as you come to a busy road for example, and when it is time to play or run off lead in a safe area.

So, it is important to teach this from the moment that you start teaching your dog anything new at all. The release command is, as mentioned in a previous chapter, a word or words that you use at the end of each session or piece of training to let him know the training has finished. This can be, 'finished', 'all over', 'training over', or something similar. But again please be consistent here with the term you use.

Some people will prefer to issue the release command at the end of each piece of training so that the dog/puppy doesn't become bored with a lot of discipline. This may be necessary in the early stages, and will ensure the puppy remains focused. Others will simply issue the final release command after your training session is complete.

b.) Sit

For the dog that sits naturally, it is simple to capture the behavior with a click (or "good boy/girl"). Whilst it is also possible to easily lure the act, so that the dog is in the sit position.

This is a position that comes so naturally to a dog that most Bichon Frisé dogs, as they are so naturally intelligent, will pop into the sit position if you show them something that they want.

As previously noted, this command is the best one to start with because sitting is a natural behavior your dog performs anyway. All you have to do is teach him to do it on command.

To teach your dog to sit on command, follow these steps:

1. Kneel in front of your Bichon Frisé and hold a small treat in your dominant hand. Pinch the treat between your thumb and forefinger so your puppy can see it.

2. Hold the treat directly in front of your Bichon Frisé's nose and give him a second to smell it.

3. Say "Sit" in a firm and even tone then immediately move the treat forward, away from you, toward the back of your dog's head. I prefer to keep saying the word sit until he sits. This is a technique

known as leading, in that you lead your dog to perform the required action.

4. Your dog should lift his nose to follow the treat and, in doing so, his bottom should lower to the floor.

5. As soon as your dog's bottom hits the ground, click with your clicker or praise him excitedly with good boy/girl to mark the 'sit' behavior and finally give him the treat.

6. Quickly release your dog, (remember the release word previously noted) repeat and practice.

7. Repeat this sequence several times until your puppy gets the hang of it.

8. Once your puppy does get the hang of the sequence, you should not have to lead anymore and just say 'sit' and he should sit.

9. If after all this, you find that he doesn't seem to be getting the idea, you can apply gentle pressure to the top of his hips, all the while saying 'sit'. This should hopefully encourage him to sit down.

10. Gradually increase the time between command, act and click/reward delivery. In this way he will retain focus longer and longer, until you finally give him the reward.

Teaching a Bichon Frisé to sit in this way will probably take 1 to 3 training sessions in a quiet area then it will need practice in various areas. Gradually increase distractions, to become a flawless command.

c.) Down

Teaching a dog to lie down is another useful command. This can be used for anything from settling your dog when visitors come to the home, right through to telling him to drop at distance in an emergency.

The easiest way to teach a dog the down position initially is to lure the position. After a few goes, he will be offering to get into the position very quickly if he thinks you have something he may want.

What you are effectively doing is to take a treat and pop it onto the end of your dog's nose and lure him to the ground. Here, you are drawing the treat down to the ground. It usually works in between his legs or as near as.

Again, once you have taught your Bichon Frisé to sit, teaching him to lie down is the next logical step.

To teach your dog to lie down on command, follow these steps:

1. Kneel in front of your Bichon Frisé and hold a small treat in your dominant hand. Pinch the treat between your thumb and forefinger so your puppy can see it.

2. Hold the treat directly in front of your Bichon Frisé's nose and give him a second to smell it.

3. Give your puppy the "Sit" command and wait for him to comply.

4. Once your puppy sits, immediately move the treat quickly down to the floor in between your puppy's front paws. It is important at this point to add the word "Down", or "Lie Down". I often prefer to keep repeating the word "Down", so that he hears it often enough to know that this new action relates to the word.

5. Your puppy should lie down to get the treat. The instant he does, again mark this with a click or praise him excitedly and give him the treat.

6. If your puppy stands up instead of lying down, calmly return to the beginning and repeat the sequence.

7. Again, once he successfully carries out the command, quickly release your dog, (remember the release word previously noted) repeat and practice.

8. Repeat this sequence several times until your puppy gets the hang of it.

9. You should be able to get to the point of skipping the 'sit' command and simply say 'Lie Down', to get the desired action from him.

There are some extra options for the dog that is simply not getting the idea. You can sit on a chair and lure your Bichon Frisé under your outstretched leg. What this does is to make him crawl under your leg, which should leave him in the down position.

Be patient here, but if after countless attempts, nothing seems to be working then try the following. As you go through the sequence above, if his back end is sticking up in a beg position, gently apply some pressure to his hips. As you gently push down say the words, 'down' or 'lie down'. Again, as soon as he does it, and doesn't immediately get up, click or praise to mark the behavior and reward.

Teaching a Bichon Frisé to lie down will usually take 3 to 6 short training sessions in a quiet area. You will then need to practice in various areas, gradually increasing distractions, to become a flawless command.

d) Come

Teaching your dog to come to you when called is incredibly important. Say, for instance, that you open the front door of your house one day and your Bichon Frisé rushes out before you can stop him. Your dog does not understand the danger of a busy street but if you have taught him to come to you when called, you can save him from that danger. In an emergency situation, your down command or the stay command will come in very handy. Using either one of those will hopefully stop him in his tracks. You can then call him back and away from any danger.

The Bichon Frisé needs to be taught to come back when called as soon as possible and in careful stages.

Most dogs can either be super responsive to recall or happy to leave you standing all day, calling his name in vain, whilst he chases rabbits or squirrels around the park. Regardless of his behavior outdoors though, this breed really needs a free run every day in order to be truly healthy.

Even the very best behaved pet that is happy to settle in the home, whether he has been for a run or not, will suffer if he isn't given the opportunity to stretch his muscles. A bored Bichon Frisé dog can easily become depressed, destructive or even aggressive.

Owners give many reasons for not giving a Bichon Frisé the free run that he needs, most of the reasons are fear in one way or another. The main concern is that the dog owner is scared of their pet running away and never coming back.

Recall training can be broken down into easy steps and recall games added to strengthen the behavior. The exact same approach is taken when teaching recall as when teaching anything else to the dog. You always set the dog up to succeed; never allow room for failure; therefore building his confidence high.

With recall you need to make certain that your dog sees you as the most interesting and attractive prospect in the area. If you are red faced and shouting his name with frustration he is less likely to want to come back. He will naturally think you are angry with him.

There are some very specific habits that you can procure when teaching recall;

Ideally you should allow your dog off the lead to run or do recall training in an isolated area and certainly not near a busy road were there is a risk of him running across the road and possibly being run over. Please do remember that Bichon Frisés do have a reputation to take off after rabbits, and some generally run away. Always be on your guard to potentially hazardous areas and therefore avoid accidents. I once had a situation with an Irish Setter that took off across a field, after she had picked up the scent of something. I literally shouted my head off and fortunately she came to her senses and came running back. Dogs can easily give chase to rabbits and if you are near a road there is a chance the rabbit may cross, along with your dog. Please preempt and avoid this from happening. If in doubt, keep your dog on a long 5 or 10 meter training type lead.

If you get a situation as described above, never punish your dog when he gets to you. Always be welcoming and friendly, no matter how frustrated you are, or he may not come back at all next time.

Never chase your dog. The only time you should give chase is if an emergency situation is apparent. If possible run the other way if he is ignoring you. By being the most interesting thing in the area and rapidly disappearing into the distance you are most likely to attract the attention of your Bichon Frisé. Giving chase can be seen as a game for the dog and you giving chase adds to their excitement.

Set up positive results. When your dog is looking for the next thing to do this is the best time to call him and show the treat. Yes, it's trickery but it will convince the dog that he comes to you each time you call.

Whether your dog is ten weeks or ten years old, puppy recall steps will work in the same way.

For complete success it is vital not to move on from the present step unless it is absolutely 100% learned and established. Remember we are aiming for success even if we have to manipulate it at first.

Whether you have never allowed your dog off his leash or he runs away every time you do, these stages will help. It is much better to go too slowly though. You want to avoid giving your dog the idea of running away.

To teach your dog to come to you on command, follow these steps:

1. Work out an extra motivator involving your clicker and some tasty treats of course. Also carry a squeaky toy or something of equal fascination to your dog. Save the toy for recall and only allow short play periods and limited use by your dog. This will ensure that it is a "magic toy" in his mind. Again, the thing to bare in mind is that it needs to make him keen enough to want it.

2. I would always advise you to do this in a secluded open field, preferably away from any road. You may have success with this in a secluded part of a park field, perhaps early morning. It is also a great idea as previously mentioned, to get hold of one of those long retractable leads or a 10 meter plus training lead. That way you can let him off at some distance, but you still have him safely attached, in case he decides to take off.

3. Now simply let him go off, all the while allowing the lead to extend. Stop, and call him back with your recall command (I would advise using his name along with 'come' or 'come on' or 'come here'). The moment he is heading back towards you use a click/praise then take his collar and give him the treat, and always use the release command.

4. It is vital to take the dog's collar every time you give him the treat because this

prevents the act of 'grab and run'. Do not be tempted to ask your dog to sit or do anything else at this point, he came to you and this is enough for now, adding extra commands is adding pressure to the recall command and may put your dog off.

5. Only when your dog is coming back every single time using the extended leash, enlist the help of a friend. Your helper is going to hold your dog and you are going to show the dog a treat. Take a few steps away and call the dog. Your helper is then going to release him as you call. As he runs toward you, click/praise, take his collar and treat in exactly the same way. Release him as before.

6. Then, when the above steps are established you can increase the distance that you go before the dog is released. You can start to run away and hide. Eventually you can start to allow the dog off leash and practice calling him back a few times each walk.

This whole process may take a few weeks but do not be tempted to let your dog off the long leash too soon as he may ignore your call and this can easily develop into a habit of running away.

E.) STAY

After you have taught your dog to come to you on command, the next logical step is to teach him to stay or wait until you call him.

To teach your dog to stay on command, follow these steps:

1. Kneel in front of your Bichon Frisé and hold a small treat in your dominant hand. Pinch the treat between your thumb and forefinger so your puppy can see it.

2. Hold the treat directly in front of your Bichon Frisé's nose and give him a second to smell it.

3. Give your puppy the "Sit" command and wait for him

to comply.

4. Now say "Stay" in a firm, even tone and take a step or two backward away from your puppy.

5. Pause for a second then walk back up to your puppy. Now click/praise to mark the fact that he has stayed put. Finally reward him with a treat. You do not want to release him until you have walked back and he has successfully remained seated throughout.

6. Repeat the sequence several times, rewarding your puppy each time he stays.

Each time you practice this, aim to increase the distance between you and your dog. You can measure this in paces if you like, so two steps to four, then eight and so on. Once I get some distance between me and the dog, I like to add the release so that he comes back to me. So start him in the sit position as before and say 'stay'. I usually keep repeating this as I walk backward. Once you have walked back quite a few paces, stop and pause as long as you feel he is concentrating. Then call him back to you, with 'come on [his name]', praise and give him the treat as before.

f.) Heel

Teaching a Bichon Frisé to heel is easy. Or it should be if you have been using this initially when you started his general walk. I always teach walking to heel with him on a leash first then off leash in a safe area. To a certain extent, you will probably have already introduced him to this in the early training as mentioned previously when you started him on his walks. We will extend and add to that training here.

When you are teaching a dog to walk to heel it is important that you focus on the position and never on the leash.

To keep pulling the dog back from a tense leash, to a slack one, whilst stating the command to heel will never work, or may turn into a form of harsh training, which we want to avoid. The dog is not actually learning anything positive with this approach.

Training Steps;

» Some people prefer to start the puppy in a sit, stay position, and then move to either the right or left hand side of the dog.

» It is important that you have the loop of the lead through whichever is your preferred lead hand, so it hangs on your wrist. Your puppy should then be on the opposite side to that. So if you hold the loop of the lead in your right hand, have the dog walk at your left side. This is more for control and safety of your puppy in these initial stages. With the other hand, in this case your left, grip the lead, so that it is close to your dog, again giving you greater control. This will also act as a guide or restraint to let your puppy know where you want him, should your puppy surge forward or hang back.

» Next give the command to "heel", whilst starting to walk. Hopefully your puppy will follow you at your side. All the while say the command "heel", not just once, but keep repeating this.

» If at this point your puppy has walked with you, without surging in front or lagging behind, and staying at your side; then you can stop click/praise to mark the behavior and again give him his treat. That is the ideal scenario. However if he doesn't do that, simply stop and start again.

» Remember, at whatever point he successfully walks at heel and you have praised him, release him before you continue. Once again, only release him, off lead, in a safe area. If you are doing this training by a roadside, by all means use the release command, but always retain control with the lead.

» Now do exactly as before, only this time try and go further, perhaps walking several feet or yards. Again stop when you are satisfied he has improved and as before, click/praise, reward and release.

» Eventually you will have him walking nicely at your side without pulling forward or holding back.

» When you've completed the session, praise your dog with your usual release command, indicating that you have finished, so that he understands he has been successful, you are pleased and that training is over.

» Once again, when training a young puppy who pulls strongly at the leash, you'll need to stand still until your pup understands that he's not going anywhere until he listens. Once your puppy understands that he only receives praise when he begins to respond appropriately, it will only take a few days before he's walking right next to you without pulling on the lead.

» Once you get him successfully walking at your side, you can increase the difficulty of the exercise by suddenly turning at a right angle, or do a complete about turn. This is more or less what happens in agility training and dog shows. The dog follows precise paths at your side.

» As mentioned at the beginning, you can increase the level of difficulty with this exercise by eventually practicing this without the lead. However, only try this in a safe area, and certainly not near a busy road.

Teaching a Bichon Frisé to walk nicely at heel will probably take 4 to 6 training sessions in a quiet area. It will then need practice in various areas, gradually increasing distractions, to become a flawless command.

If you follow the steps listed previously, teaching your puppy to respond to the five basic commands should not be a difficult or lengthy process. Make sure to keep your training sessions short. Only about 10 or 15 minutes to ensure that your puppy stays engaged. If he starts to get bored or distracted in the middle of a session, stop for now and pick it up again later.

3) Phasing Out Food Rewards

Food is a highly motivating reward for dogs. But you do not want your Bichon Frisé to become dependent on a food reward indefinitely to perform the desired behavior. Once your puppy starts to respond consistently with the right behavior, when you give him a command, you should start phasing out the treats. Start by only rewarding your puppy every other time then cut it back to every third time and so on. Even though you are phasing out the food rewards you still need to praise your puppy so he knows that you are pleased with him. You may even choose to substitute a food reward for a toy and give your puppy a brief play session with the toy as a reward instead of the treat. Do not feel guilty that your poor dog is looking sad, disappointed and bewildered by no longer receiving his treat. All dogs are only too happy to please their owner, and he will soon get used to no longer getting the treat every time. Of course you are free to treat your dog occasionally. But you are doing his long time health no favors by constantly giving him treats. Also please be aware that there are dog trainers who do not use treats at all and successfully train happy dogs.

4) Discipline Whilst Training.

We have now talked a lot about positive reinforcement training,as opposed to any punishment based methods. I always advocate a firm but fair approach and dislike the idea of 'disciplining' a dog. But it is worth clarifying your approach to training. Most dogs behave perfectly well and respect you as their carer. Some dogs however, can have a willful personality and they will sometimes test you and misbehave. Again, I would never advocate hitting a dog nor would I advocate being a strict disciplinarian for the sake of it. But if your puppy does appear to be developing willful disobedience, the following will be worth bearing in mind.

1) Remember a well behaved adult is the result of a correctly trained puppy, given firm basic training.

2) Your dog will respect you when you are firm but fair, and when you say 'No', they should know this by your tone of voice. You obviously do not want to become a sergeant major, barking commands. But if say for example, you tell your dog to stay or wait and he starts to move before you have given the word, then tell him in a slightly disapproving voice, 'No'.

Do not feel bad, or that you are being cruel and do not forget that this training could potentially save your dogs life in an emergency situation. In this respect, I would not advise shouting at your dog whilst generally training your puppy. However, if you are in an emergency situation shouting may be the only way to shock or frighten your puppy into realizing something is seriously wrong. If you shout all the time, he will probably see this as normal, and be unable or unlikely to differentiate when something is seriously wrong.

Sometimes he will need to know that he is doing wrong with a firm 'No'. It will be even more satisfying to him, when you shower him with praise. Also remember some personalities need and respect someone who they take as a strong leader. Again, without wishing to get into a debate about 'alpha dog' training, dogs generally respect you when you are firm but fair.

Chapter Seven:

Grooming Your Bichon Frisé

Grooming your Bichon Frisé is very important. Not only does grooming help to control shedding but it also helps to ensure that your dog's coat and skin remain healthy. In this chapter you will learn the basics about grooming your Bichon Frisé including tips for cleaning your dog's ears and trimming his nails. Please be aware that this is the one aspect of the Bichon Frisé that is relatively demanding and time consuming. It is also very important that regular grooming is applied. Grooming doesn't have to take over your life, it depends on whether you want a show dog look or a pet trim. Either way, daily brushing is highly recommended.

1) Grooming and Parasites:

Before we get into the actual grooming and bathing, it is worth mentioning parasites that you may encounter whilst grooming. We will talk more about parasites in another chapter, but as you are most likely to notice fleas and tics etc, whilst grooming we will discuss dealing with those here. Fleas, tics and mites are the most likely culprits you will encounter. Fleas prefer to bury and hide themselves in a relatively thick coat such as a Bichon Frisé .

The added problem with fleas, is that they can also set up home in the dogs bedding or the furnishings of your home. It is therefore necessary to not only treat the dog, but their bedding and your furnishings. If you ever get a particularly bad infestation, it may be necessary to call in professional pest controllers. I have never had to experience this, but have had experience with a minor infestation. I found that fumigating the house with a good smoke bomb did the trick. All I then had to do was to keep on top of any fleas invading either the dog or house with the occasional flea spray or powder on the bedding, and a number of remedies on the dog.

It is up to you what remedies you use on your dog. So called 'spot on' treatments are commonly recommended by vets. They do work, but a lot of dog owners, who are more organically inclined, are against the idea of applying these because of a potential toxic effect to the dog. It is not for me to comment about the long term effect of any such toxins to the future health of the dog. What I have also noticed is that long time market leaders such as Frontline have recently been proved to not be as affective as they once were. The vet that I currently use recommends a product called Stronghold as a much better alternative. I have to say that I have used this product and it does seem to work, with only the occasional flea showing up. My dogs appear perfectly healthy, vital and seemingly unaffected by this product. I hasten to add here, that I am in no way recommending nor endorsing any product, but am merely speaking about veterinary advice I have been given and personal experience. Other vets or individuals may well disagree with this information.

2.)Grooming Tools and Methods

IMPORTANT: Please note that it is highly recommended that you remove any matted hair or tangles before bathing. An experienced groomer will tell you that it is almost impossible to remove mats and tangles once wet. Quite often cutting wet tangles out is the only option. A professional groomer may have more success by spraying anti tangle/ de-matting solution, if the dog is wet. But again this is all avoided if you take the time to properly brush and comb the coat, before the bath.

You have already learned that it is recommended you have your Bichon Frisé professionally groomed every 4 to 6 weeks, but you should still perform regular brushing and bathing at home. Again, the best tools to use in brushing your Bichon Frisé are a wire pin brush/bristle brush, slicker brush, and fine and wide-tooth combs. When you brush your Bichon Frisé, start at the head and brush gently in the direction of hair growth, then again in the opposite direction, against the lay. Work your way down the dog's neck, along his back, and down his legs. Do not forget the chest and neck.

If you encounter any tangles or mats while brushing your Bichon Frisé you can use the wide-tooth comb to carefully work them out. If you are unable to work the tangle free, use anti tangle solution. If all else fails, you can use a small pair of sharp scissors to cut it out. When cutting out a mat, pinch the dog's fur between the skin and the mat when you cut to make sure you don't accidentally cut your dog's skin.

Some dogs do not react well to grooming because they do not like being held still. Because grooming is so important for Bichon Frisés, you should get your puppy used to grooming from an early age. Brush your puppy for a few seconds at a time several times a day until he no longer seems bothered by it. Then you can cut back to one longer brushing session each day. You should also frequently touch your puppy's paws and ears so that once you start trimming his nails and cleaning his ears he will be used to this kind of handling.

Grooming your Bichon Frisé is a relatively easy, if not time consuming process.

The general procedure is as follows.

1. Using the bristle/pin brush first of all, give a good all round brush. Carefully draw the brush with the lay of the coat, then against the lay.
2. Now with the slicker brush give a more thorough brushing. Again, carefully draw the brush with the lay, then against the lay of the coat. You will find loose hair gathers, which you should remove as it builds up on the brush.
3. Once the hair is sufficiently loosened, the next step is to use the wide toothed comb to comb through the coat. The idea is to tidy the coat, but also remove any tangles. Hopefully there wont be any, but if so, be careful here not to pull the coat and hurt your dog. Always hold the tangled hair with one hand and then attempt to comb out any tangles. Again, sometimes it is necessary to cut out tangles, but you should only do this as a last resort. As previously mentioned, professional groomers generally recommend untangle sprays.

Bichon Frisés are generally a clean breed but they do need bathing occasionally, especially if they spend a lot of time outside.

To bathe your Bichon Frisé at home follow the steps outlined below:

3) Bathing your Bichon Frisé

As a matter of routine, I always use an old towel to dry my dogs legs and feet, on damp, wet outings. You will usually find that this sufficiently dries and cleans any soiled areas.

If you have to wash mud from their legs, feet or coat, please do this with warm water, but no shampoo. You can then either towel dry and or use a hair drier to ensure your dog does not get chilled.

Avoid bathing your dog on a regular basis as this strips the skin and coat of natural healthy oils. Remember that your Bichon Frisé's skin has a pH of around 7.5, while humans have a pH of 5.5. That said, never use human shampoo on your Bichon Frisé. This will lead to scaling and skin irritation. There are numerous dog shampoos available for various canine skin problems. It is also advisable to use a good conditioner. Some groomers will also recommend adding a T spoon of baby oil to the conditioner. This helps to to stop the coat and skin from drying out, which is obviously important for Bichon's due to regular bathing.

Don't forget that your dog relies on natural oils to keep the skin soft, healthy and free from drying out. The oil also has the benefit of protecting the coat and retaining its water resistance. It is tempting to consider how grubby and uncomfortable us humans feel when we don't bathe regularly. However, you cannot take that same viewpoint where your dog is concerned.

To bathe your Bichon Frisé at home follow the steps outlined below:

1. Give your Bichon Frisé a good brushing, as above, before you bathe him to get rid of accumulated loose hair.
2. Fill your bathtub with a few inches of lukewarm water. You may also want to put down a bath mat so your dog doesn't slip in the tub.
3. Place your Bichon Frisé in the tub and wet down his fur with a handheld hose or by pouring water over him. Because the Bichon Frisé's coat is relatively long, you may need to use your hands to work the water all the way down to his skin.
4. Avoid getting your Bichon Frisé's eyes and ears wet when you bathe him. Wet ears are a breeding ground for bacteria that could cause an ear infection.
5. Apply a small amount of mild dog-friendly shampoo to your Bichon Frisé's back and gently work it into a lather along his neck, back, chest and legs.
6. Rinse the soap thoroughly out of your Bichon Frisé's coat and use a damp washcloth to clean his face.

7. Use a large fluffy towel to towel-dry your Bichon Frisé, getting as much water out of his coat as possible.

You can bathe your Bichon Frisé if he gets dirty, but you should avoid bathing him when it is not necessary. Again, over-bathing a dog can dry out his skin and lead to skin problems. In some cases you may be able to brush dried dirt and debris out of your Bichon Frisé's coat instead of bathing him.

4) Blow drying

You will no doubt have to blow dry the coat after their bath. If you use your own hair dryer, be careful that this is not at its highest hot setting. It is advisable to brush the coat as you blow dry and proceed as follows:

1. You will use the bristle/pin brush first, giving the coat a good brush. The slicker will pull the coat much more initially, so you should use the slicker after the bristle/pin brushing. You then do exactly the same with the slicker brush to get a more pronounced 'powder puff/boufant' look. As you brush, go with the lay of the coat firstly to loosen the hair, then against the lay to obtain the powder puff look. Concentrate on small sections and work systematically from the tail. You should continuously brush as you blow dry. Please be careful not to pull the coat as you brush. A professional groomer will have a hair dryer on a stand, therefore leaving both hands free. One hand will brush the coat, whilst the other will hold the coat taut in the opposite direction to brushing, and so avoid pulling the skin. Without the hairdryer on a stand, I have to say, the best alternative method is for you have an assistant help you.
2. Now use the same technique on the legs
3. Next brush and blow dry the body
4. Lastly brush and blow the head and ears.

If you would prefer to see this whole process on video, please search [blow drying a bichon] on YouTube. Please note that the whole blow drying process is likely to take between 25 and 30 minutes. Once you have brushed and blow dried, you are ready to trim.

5) Hair Trimming.

When trimming your Bichon you can do a simple pet trim using a combination of electric clippers and scissors. Electric clippers do provide an easy way to get a relatively uniform look as you simply follow the contours of your dogs legs and body. The disadvantage, is that you are generally limited to the length you can cut. Many professional groomers prefer to trim free hand with scissors as you generally get a more fuller look. It is entirely up to you which method you adopt. Your best bet for a trimming guideline is to copy as near as possible a typical Bichon Frisé powder puff cut, similar to the examples below.

You are basically aiming for a rounded look that leaves approximately 1 to 2 inches of hair all round, but obviously this will be closer if clippers are used.

For a trim using scissors, please proceed as follows:

1. Once your dog is properly blow dried, you will need to thoroughly comb the coat. The key here is to comb the hair up away from the lay of the coat as opposed to combing it flat.
2. If the ears are overly thick and fluffy it may be necessary to thin the hair with a pair of thinning scissors. When trimming the flap of the ear itself be very careful that you can see the skin of the ear, as you obviously want to avoid accidentally cutting the ear.
3. Trim excess hair from under the feet, again be very careful not to cut the skin.
4. Trim the hair around the anus in the same manner
5. The tail hair should be left relatively long, so only trim a small amount from the length.
6. The rear needs to have a rounded look with the legs cylindrical. It is advisable when trimming the legs and body to keep the scissors parallel to the standing surface or parallel to the dogs body
7. Now trim the body hair starting at the top and moving down and underneath. When trimming underneath, it may be necessary to get someone to hold your dog in a standing upright posi-

tion, so you can easily trim the hair. Again, aim for a consistent look that retains the contours but also has the puffed out look.

8. The front should look straighter less rounded than the rear, but to still retain the cylindrical look.
9. Be careful when trimming around the eyes. You firstly comb the hair forward over the eyes and then trimmed back so the top of the eyes are showing. Any hair around the eyes should be carefully trimmed.
10. Comb the hair along the bridge of the nose towards the tip of the nose. Comb the hair of the muzzle downwards and trim any excess.
11. The beard should be trimmed in line with the ends of the ears.

That is a very brief step by step trimming guideline. Once again, if you are unsure, always get a professional groomer to guide you in the first instance. You can also view some very good videos on YouTube by typing in the search term, [Bichon Frisé Trimming], or something similar.

6) Trimming Your Dog's Nails

Trimming your Bichon Frisé's nails can be challenging because you need to be very careful. A dog's nail contains a quick; the vessel that brings blood to the nail. If you cut the nail too short you will cut the quick. This not only causes your dog pain, but it can bleed profusely as well. When you trim your Bichon Frisé's nails you should only cut the very tip to remove the point. Depending on what color your dog's nails are, you may be able to see the quick and use it as a trimming guide.

It is generally recommended that you trim your Bichon Frisé's nails every two weeks. If you do it this often then you will only need to clip the slightest amount off the nail each time. This will reduce the risk of cutting the quick. Before you trim your Bichon Frisé's nails for the first time you should consider having a veterinarian or a professional groomer show you how. You also need to be sure you are using real dog nail clippers for the job. Please also be aware that you shouldn't attempt to clip your dog's nails routinely every two weeks, just for the sake of it, as he may not need it. You should notice that if your dog walks on pavements or your concrete yard, he will to a certain extent be filing them down anyway.

7) Cleaning Your Dog's Ears

Because the Bichon Frisé's ears hang down over the sides of his head there is an increased risk of ear infections. Drop ears, results in air and moisture being trapped under the flap of the ear, making it a breeding ground for bacteria. Your dog's risk for ear infection increases significantly if you get the ears wet, such as during a bath.

Cleaning your dog's ears is not difficult, but you do need the right supplies. Gear up with a bottle of dog-friendly ear cleaning solution and a few clean cotton balls. Gently lift your dog's ear and squeeze a few drops of the cleaning solution into the ear canal. Rub the base of your dog's ear with your fingers to spread the solution then use the cotton balls to wipe it away. Be careful not to put your fingers or the cotton ball too far into your dog's ear or you could damage his ear drum. The frequency with which you clean your Bichon Frisé's ears will vary, but you should aim for once every week or two.

8) Brushing Your Bichon Frisé's Teeth

Please be aware that if you adopt the type of diet advocated by vets such as Ian Billinghurst, this next step is likely to be unnecessary. If however, you feed a commercial feed, particularly kibble, then this next section may be necessary. The idea of brushing your dog's teeth may sound strange but dental health is just as important for your dog as it is for you. In fact, periodontitis (gum disease) is five times more common in dogs than in humans. Gum disease is incredibly serious but it often goes unnoticed by pet parents, especially since many people think that dogs are supposed to have bad breath. Bad breath, or halitosis, is one of the most common signs of gum disease and could be indicative of a tooth abscess. Once again, please note that dogs regularly chewing on suitable raw meaty bones have relatively odourless breath. If you suspect an abscess, or anything un-toward, seek a veterinary examination as soon as possible.

To brush your Bichon Frisé's teeth, follow the steps below:

» Select a soft-bristle toothbrush to use. Most pet stores stock special toothbrushes for dogs.

» Choose a toothpaste that is specifically made for dogs, never human tooth paste. They come in a variety of flavors, so select one your Bichon Frisé will like. He will probably like them all. Again, never use the tooth paste you use. These contain chemicals that can be harmful to dogs.

» Get your dog used to having his teeth handled by gently placing your finger in his mouth against his teeth. Carefully manipulate his lips so he gets used to the feeling.

» If you find he doesn't particularly like this, try dipping your finger in peanut butter or chicken broth so your dog learns to like the treatment.

» When you are ready to brush, place one hand over your dog's mouth and gently pull back his lips.

» Apply a small amount of toothpaste to the brush and rub it gently over a few of his teeth.

» After a few seconds, stop brushing and give your Bichon Frisé a treat for good behavior.

» Slowly increase the length of your brushing sessions over a few days until your dog lets you brush all of his teeth in one session.

» In addition to brushing your Bichon Frisé's teeth at home you should also make sure he gets a dental check-up from the vet every 6 months.

9) DEALING WITH EYE STAINS

Dogs with light-colored fur like the Bichon Frisé tend to develop discolored stains in the corners of their eyes. This is common and generally not a problem unless the discharge is yellow or green and if it has an unpleasant odor. These may be signs of infection. If you suspect that your Bichon Frisé has an eye infection you should take him to the vet immediately.

Otherwise, follow the steps below to clean away eye stains:

» Mix one part hydrogen peroxide with 10 parts fresh water in a small container.

» Dip a clean cotton swab into the solution and rub it gently into the fur around your dog's eyes to remove stains. Be very careful not to get any of the solution into your dog's eyes.

» Use a clean cloth or cotton ball to dry the area after you have removed the stains.

» Add one teaspoon of distilled white vinegar or apple cider vinegar to your dog's drinking water. This will change the pH of the water and help to prevent bacterial growth that leads to staining.

» Keep the fur around your dog's eyes trimmed short. If the hair gets into your dog's eyes it could cause irritation leading to excessive tearing.

In most cases, tear staining in Bichon Frisés is not a serious problem. It can affect the way your dog looks but it may not be the result of a medical problem. If your dog's tearing becomes excessive or recurrent, take your dog to the vet to identify and treat the underlying cause.

CHAPTER EIGHT:

HEALTH CHECKS AND FIRST AID

Before we get into the main health issues affecting the Bichon Frisé, this chapter will deal with important preventive care. There is also useful and sometimes vital advice on health checks and first aid.

1.) CHOOSING A VETERINARIAN

You may already know this but not all veterinarians are the same. They are only people after all. So to find a good vet that you get on well with, may take some time and effort.

It is vitally important that you are completely happy with the vet that you choose for your dog. This person may need to lead you through some very difficult times. So a veterinarian who is hazy when sharing information or blunt towards you, may be very stressful for your entire family if you have an ill dog.

A good way to find a popular vet in your local area is do some community research, ask other dog walkers, go onto Facebook and find community pages of dog owners in your local area. Find out from other people what their experiences are and learn from them.

2.) DAILY HEALTH CHECK: ESSENTIAL HANDLING

You will get used to seeing your new friend on a daily basis and quickly get used to his quarks and how he generally behaves. It will therefore become very obvious to you if something is wrong health wise. If you suspect that your dog is ill, just remember that most serious illnesses occur simultaneously with a rise in body temperature. It therefore makes sense to take your dogs temperature, which if you havn't already got one, please do get a rectal thermometer. If your dog is used to standing, you can probably do this yourself by holding his tail and with a small amount of vaseline or similar, insert the thermometer into his rectum. If he wont stand for you doing this, then you will need someone to help you hold him whilst you insert the thermometer

A normal average temperature for a dog should be about 101.5 °F (38.6°C). If there is a rise of even a few degrees and this isn't the result of a sudden burst of exercise or similar, then assume there is a problem and consult with your vet a.s.a.p.

Preventative Care

From the very minute that you purchase your Bichon Frisé puppy, you will be responsible for his care. The only way to tell if your Bichon Frisé is becoming ill, is to be in tune with him. You'll need to take a few minutes each day to do simple health checks. Some of these can be done while grooming, such as feeling for bumps or loss of muscle.

You will no doubt be able to see if your puppy or adult dog, looks ill, or seems weak and listless for no reason.

Daily examinations will include examinations for:

» Bleeding, swollen, or pale gums, loose or broken teeth, mouth ulcers, or bad breath

» Discharge from the eyes or nose

» Ears having a bad odor, redness or discharge

» The skin for parasites, hair loss, hot spots, crusts or lumps

» The feet for abrasions, bleeding, broken nails or misaligned toes

What Will Early Handling Establish

Handling your dog early on will teach him that being touched and health checked is a perfectly normal part of his life. This makes life so much easier at the vets along with making nail clipping and similar activities stress free. Handling in this way will also give you the chance to see what is normal for your own dog and his health. This way you will be able to recognize and catch any problems quickly.

Physical Manipulation

If you live with a young puppy, lift the dog up and cradle him in your arms on his back. There is no real reason for this position other than it's quite a difficult place for a dog to relax in, because it exposes his belly. Therefore by enjoying it, he is learning to be relaxed when handled regardless of what is going on. You will probably not be able to manage this with older Bichon Frisés. In this case you should really just attempt handling in whatever position is comfortable for them, whether sitting or lying them down on their back, or front. The important thing is that you handle them. Also be initially wary of an older rescue dog until you know that they do not mind you handling them.

Next, take hold of each paw and look at the underside of the pads by squashing them open. This will help to check pads for cuts and foreign articles when you really need to. If you find any sharp object stuck in there, do your best to carefully pull this out preferably with tweezers. If this looks difficult, then you are probably best taking him to the vet, as soon as possible, to get them to extract it.

Ears

Take a good look into the dog's ears. They should be pink and clean with no thick or smelly discharge. Look out for signs of redness and swelling.

Try to make the ear examination similar to one he will have at the veterinary surgery. Again if you notice anything untoward, do not delay in taking him to the vet.

Eyes

Carefully examine your dog's eyes for swelling or redness. A small amount of sleep is normal. If you live with an adult or an older dog any blueness or blurring can be a sign of cataracts.

You can check your dog's sight by holding his face gently forward and dropping a balled up tissue or feather on the edge of his vision at each side of his head. If his vision is fine he will notice this straight away, if not, he may have a problem. Again a trip to the vets will be best for further investigation.

http://www.vetstreet.com/care/the-ophthalmic-exam

Teeth

Next check your dog's teeth right to the back of his mouth. As previously mentioned, it is a good idea to start brushing your dog's teeth early. If you are doing this on a daily basis, you will soon notice any problems that will need checking at the vets.

http://www.animalwellness-magazine.com/articles/alternative-dental-care/

Dental sticks are often used and are supposed to do a similar job to brushing. However, be careful as some contain sugar, and as well as being bad for the teeth and gums can add to your dog becoming overweight. Many people swear by fresh bones, but be careful not to give cooked bones as they can splinter easily and cause intestinal problems. Also it can be very painful for dogs to pass. If your dog ever suffers any problems associated with eating bones, then obviously avoid giving your dog bones. There is much debate about bone consumption for dogs. But weighing up the pros and cons, in most instances bones are probably healthier than manufactured dental sticks, if perhaps not as safe. Your dog will love them in any case, so the choice is yours.

Feet

Then check each of the paws, checking the nails, and as previously mentioned, cut any that seem to have overgrown. We have already covered this to an extent in the chapter on grooming, but it is worth mentioning again.

The toenail of a dog is slightly different to that of a human so will need very careful handling. The nerve grows into the nail, which can easily be seen with white toenails but is more difficult with dark ones.

It is completely up to you whether you clip your own dog's nails or find a professional groomer or vet to do it. If you decide to clip them, then you will need to buy specific clippers and only take the very tip away with the clippers, or you may hurt the dog. If you would like to try this yourself, but are nervous at first, ask someone to show you or watch one of the many Youtube videos for instruction.

Anus and Genitals

After the feet, simply check the anus area and genitals for any abnormal discharge or swelling then finish by physically running your hands down the puppy's tail.

a.) The Worried or Reactive Bichon Frisé

If you are bringing home an older Bichon Frisé then it is important not to push your luck with handling. Remember that the dog will be confused and maybe even quite stressed.

A good way to carry out handling with a worried dog is to do it a few minutes, or even seconds if necessary, at a time and reward with treats, then stop. The idea is to show the dog that handling and checking his ears, eyes and teeth etc, is a pleasant experience that brings nice food rewards.

Never force the worried dog beyond his limitations. Always stop whilst he is still relaxed and try to understand that this may all be brand new to him.

b.) Basic Massage and Muscle Care

Basic Massage can also be carried out when handling your dog of any age. By taking a few moments to first massage the dog's ears, where there are a lot of relaxing acupressure points, then moving your hands down his body in even strokes, you will be able to check his muscle balance and well-being.

Any uneven muscle balance will show that there is a potential skeletal problem below the surface. This is something that can be carefully monitored and should really be checked by the vet.

Any heat or swelling in the muscle areas may show a deeper problem. Similarly if the dog licks his lips, yawns or tries to move when you touch a certain area of his body, then he could have some type of pain beneath the surface and is displaying calming signals as a response to your touch. It could also be nothing to worry about and the dog displays calming signals because they perhaps do not like been handled.

3.) First Aid

As the owner of a Bichon Frisé dog it is a good idea to have at least a basic idea of canine first aid.

General first aid and its universal lesson is currently using the Acronym Dr's ABC. By memorizing this you have at least a basic idea of what to do if you ever find yourself in a first aid situation.

Danger

Remove the animal from any further danger, and be aware of danger to yourself in the situation.

Response

Check the response of the dog, is he conscious?

Summon help

Shout for help, ask someone to call the vet if possible.

Airway

Check the dog's airway, can he breathe Is there an obstruction

Breathing

At this point there may be a need to re-trigger breathing for the animal. Holding the mouth closed you can gently breath air into your dog's nostrils. Try to visualize the size of his lungs and not over inflate them, try to mimic how your dog would pant.

Cardiac compressions may be necessary at this point. The dog should be laid on his right side and the heart massaged in a similar way to CPR compressions for a human but carefully at a ratio of one breath to every two to five compressions depending on the size of the dog. The average Bichon Frisé would be around three compressions per breath. The heart is approximately located in the chest area above his front left leg. They usually have a stronger beat on the left but can be felt on both sides.

The basic sequence for CPR is as follows:

1. Check for signs of breathing which should be noticeable around the chest or by placing your cheek to your dogs mouth.
2. Check for a pulse which if this is not noticeable around the heart area, can be felt via the femoral artery. This is located on either of the back legs, on the inside of the leg, near to the top of the leg. By feeling inside that area, if there was a pulse you would feel it quite strongly there. It will be worth you detecting that now, so that you know where to look and how it should feel.
3. If neither breathing nor pulse are detected, start chest compressions. With the heel of your hand, press reasonably firmly, but in the case of the Bichon Frisé, not too firmly that you risk cracking a rib. Count about three compressions
4. Now move over to your dogs mouth/nose and steadily blow into both and you should see the chest expand.
5. Again move over to the chest and compress three times again.
6. Keep repeating the sequence until he starts to breath.

Please read the following article for additional information:

http://www.petmd.com/dog/emergency/common-emergencies/e_dg_cardiopulmonary_resuscitation

If you prefer a visual demonstration, please search Youtube using a search term such as[CPR on dogs]

Circulation

In an emergency, the dog's pulse and circulation will need to be checked. If bleeding is apparent then the wound will need to be put under pressure and elevated if possible in order to contain the bleeding.

After first aid has been carried out, the Bichon Frisé should always be taken to see the vet as a matter of urgency.

There are some particular conditions that can develop very quickly can cause rapid health deterioration; which as a Bichon Frisé owner it is important to be aware of. One of these is heat stroke or heat exhaustion.

4.) Heat Exhaustion

Dogs can only pant to cool themselves as they don't sweat like people do; except to a certain extent from their paw pads.

In the warm summer months it is vital to keep your dog away from hot sun. Because he only cools his body on the inside by taking air from his surroundings, the dog in excessive heat, loses the power to cool himself at all. This will quickly lead to heat exhaustion which can be a fatal condition.

Dogs should never be left in hot cars, full sun or hot areas from which they cannot escape.

The symptoms of heat exhaustion are as follows;

» Panting (however, dogs do this naturally anyway and in most cases is not indicative of a problem)

» Restlessness

» Loss of focus in the eyes

» Deterioration of consciousness

» Staggering

» Collapse

If you suspect that your Bichon Frisé dog is overheating it is vital never to take the panicked action of immersing him in cold water, as this can cause shock or even heart failure. Remove the dog from full sun and either drape damp towels over his body or dribble water over him to cool his overheated body gently. When the body has overheated, then it is vital to get your dog checked by the vet for symptoms of long term damage.

A relatively new invention in the dog equipment world is the cooling vest. It can be placed in water then put onto the dog in hot weather. The water wicks the heat away from the dogs body as a process of evaporation. If you believe that your dog is particularly susceptible to hot weather, then a cooling vest is a really good investment.

Another good idea for the warmer months is to provide your dog with a stock pot iced pop. Simply pour stock into a big bowl, add some treats of varying types and freeze the entire thing. Then on a hot day turn the ice pop out into the garden and allow your dog to lick away happily. You may want to place this on some sort of a tray in case the whole thing melts before he has chance to consume it.

5.) Essential Exercise

Every Bichon Frisé dog needs daily walks, and will certainly not be happy at home all day. The adult Bichon Frisé ideally needs a good walk every single day or he may develop problem behaviors. These gentle, sweet natured dogs are generally well behaved. However, excess energy build up can easily cause destructive or even aggressive behavior, to a certain extent.

Many dog behavior problems are sorted out very quickly when the dog's food is changed (food causing allergies or just poor food quality lacking necessary nutrients) and when the daily walks are increased in time and intensity. But many of the most problematic behaviors stem from a lack of suitable exercise.

If you are out at work for a full day then why not consider a doggy day care or professional dog walker for your Bichon Frisé dog. A good professional canine caretaker will wear your dog out and meet his social needs all at once.

Please be aware that Bichon Frisé puppies along with other puppy breeds, need to be broken in gently to exercise, as their bones are soft whilst they are still growing. Your regular, long walks will begin when your puppy is a few months old.

Puppy exercise should involve gentle short walks; the UK Kennel club advises;

"Puppies need much less exercise than fully-grown dogs. If you over-exercise a growing puppy you can overtire it and damage its developing joints, causing early arthritis. A good rule of thumb is a ratio of five minutes exercise per month of age (up to twice a day) until the puppy is fully grown, i.e. 15 minutes (up to twice a day) when three months old, 20 minutes when four months old etc. Once they are fully grown, they can go out for much longer.

It is important that puppies and dogs go out for exercise every day in a safe and secure area, or they may become frustrated. Time spent in the garden (however large) is no substitute for exploring new environments and socializing with other dogs. (Make sure your puppy is trained to recall so that you are confident that he will return to you when called)".

See more at: *http://www.thekennelclub.org.uk*

6.) Natural Therapy and Remedies

Natural therapy is often passed over because conventional medicine has become such a big part of our lives. This is a pity in many ways as remedies, hands on therapy and a mixture of the two can have such amazing results.

Your veterinarian can diagnose, treat with drugs and give you advice. But it is up to you then to go away and explore all of the options available to you and your dog.

In the book Veterinary Secrets: Natural Health for Dogs and Cats, (2014) Dr Andrew Jones talks through the place of veterinary medicine in the life of your dog and this book is a welcome addition to the care kit of any Bichon Frisé dog. Similarly the book The Veterinarians Guide to Natural Remedies for Dogs (2000) by Martin Zucker, is also a fantastic resource for any dog owner.

Chapter Nine

Parasites, worms and common illnesses

This chapter deals with the unfortunate subject of parasites and common illnesses that can affect your Bichon Frisé. Please do not skip this chapter as it is important that you are aware of these parasites and conditions and can therefore deal with their treatment and prevention.

1.) Parasitic Worms

A huge concern within the digestive process are parasites.

Worms are known as internal parasites of which there are plenty that can affect the Bichon Frisé dog and Bichon Frisé puppies. It may surprise you to know, but puppies are actually born with worms present. Having purchased from a reputable breeder, your puppy is bound to have already been wormed. You should check when this was, and the dose and type used, which will indicate when he needs worming next. Please do not neglect regular worming whether a puppy or adult as these parasites can seriously affect their health and in some cases lead to death. Also be very careful and stick to correct doses, as this can cause intestinal damage and again at worse lead to death.

a.) Roundworms

The most common worm type is the roundworm, of which there are a few variations. Symptoms of a roundworm infection include itchiness in the anus area, worms in the dog's feces and loss of condition.

A mother dog can pass roundworms on to her puppies and all Bichon Frisé puppies, bred and raised well, will be wormed properly by the breeder before being sent to their new homes. Worms usually live in the dog's digestive system and some are actually symptom-less, whilst others can have serious consequences for the health of the Bichon Frisé dog.

Hookworm and whipworm are also roundworm types that cause pain and digestive upset in dogs. The hookworm grips onto the stomach wall causing constant and severe discomfort to the dog.

B.) TAPEWORMS

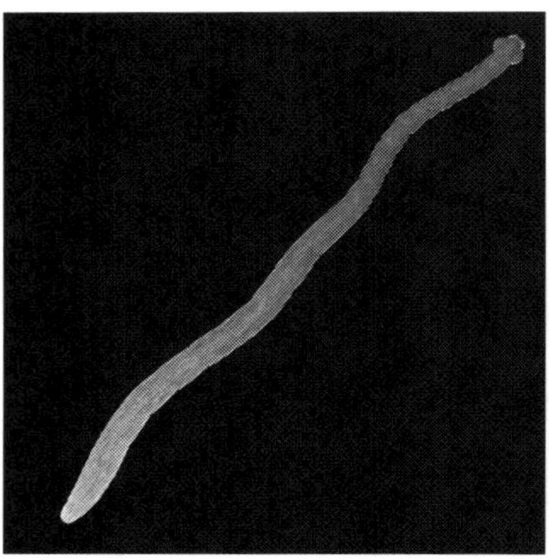

The tapeworm is a type of parasite which can sit in the intestine without doing any damage, other than consuming nutrients that your dog should be consuming. They will also grow to a large size throughout the intestinal tract. The tapeworm reproduces by shedding parts of its long and segmented body, which is passed with the feces or drops from the anus of the dog. The tapeworm is happy to live in the digestive system of both dogs and people. Again the main problem here is that it will consume a considerable amount of ingested food and obviously grow as a result. As you can imagine, your dog will not be getting sufficient nutrients and will suffer as a result.

Basic worming tablets will keep the chance of infection under control. As a routine these should be administered about every 3 months. Be careful that you are giving your dog the correct dosage. This is usually gauged by kilo weight of your dog. Also be aware that different brands suggest a different number of tablets. This is probably because of the size or potency of each tablet.

C.) LUNGWORMS/HEARTWORMS

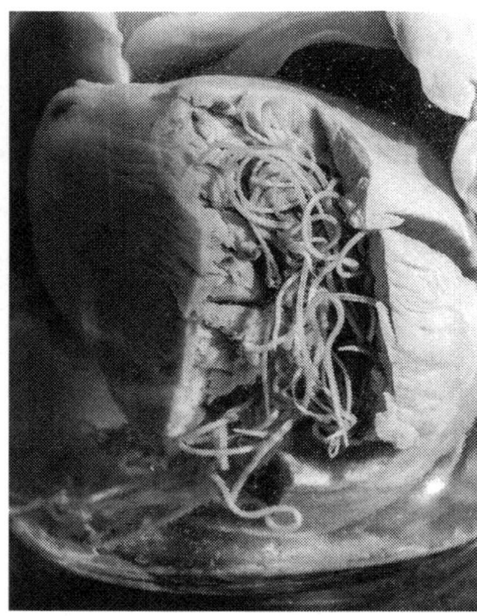

The other type of worm, and one which has serious consequences, is the lungworm/heartworm.

The larvae for this type of worm, when it gets into the body, migrates to either the lung or heart of the animal. It then quickly breeds to fill the major organ with worms, as illustated above. By the time that the symptoms of this type of infestation appears, the damage to either the heart or lungs will be well underway.

Symptoms are excessive coughing and loss of heart or lung function. This parasite type is becoming more common, and currently being diagnosed in geographical areas where it has not previously been seen.

The larvae of this parasite enters the body via a mosquito bite or ingestion. Dogs that eat slugs, snails and their eggs are particularly susceptible to an infestation of heart or lungworm.

With quick spreading infection, has come preventative medicine. If you are in an area that is high risk, I would urge you to consult with your veterinarian about preventive measures.

As a matter of routine, you are strongly advised to check with your vet, the general type of worms your dog may be susceptible to. Worming tablets can be bought at pet stores and many general stores seem to stock these now. Once again, always make sure you choose the correct type and dosage for both your dogs size and age.

2.) External Parasites - Fleas and Other Suckers

The other type of parasite that can potentially affect your Bichon Frisé dog is the external parasite.

a.) Fleas

Fleas generally seek out their host, quite often jumping from dog to dog. They then burrow within the dogs fur and feed off the dogs blood. Unfortunately they stay, reproduce and cause our dogs all sorts of problems.

Symptoms of fleas are grit like dirt that turns red in water and a profusion of itchy bites. Please remember that fleas can transmit tapeworms.

Many vets will advise that chemical treatment will need to occur every few months as a preventative measure. This is usually in the form of a spot on treatment applied to the back of the dog's neck.

Today there are advances in flea and tick control. Always contact your vet as to the best products to use. Some products are much stronger than others, so it's really important to try and choose a formula that is not harmful to your Bichon Frisé. There are plenty of flea and tick products that are natural and environmentally friendly. These will repel and kill fleas, ticks and mosquitos with a natural botanical formula like geraniol and eugenol. Sprinkling borax powder, around the home is a known flea killer. However, salt is known to do a similar job. Again, avoid direct contact of the animal as this can dry the skin and possibly have a toxic affect. Other natural remedies often recommended include lemongrass, citronella, cedar wood, neem etc. Have a look on YouTube for some useful videos on alternative natural flea remedies.

b.) Ticks

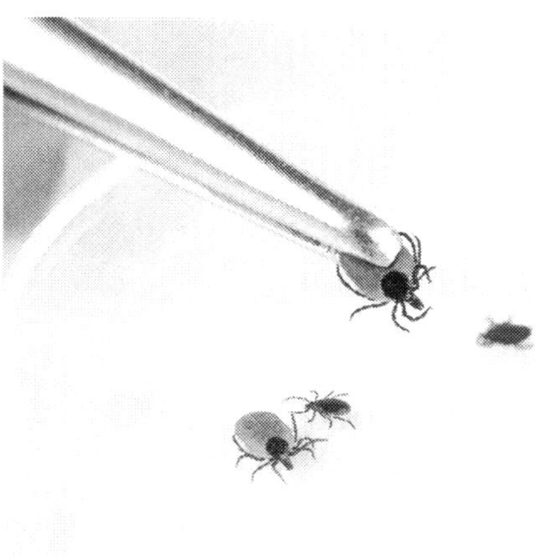

Ticks can be found anywhere on a Bichon Frisé, but are mostly found on the neck, chest, and between the toes. They are often found in the US. Ticks will transmit Rocky Mountain spotted fever, tick paralysis, Lyme disease, babesiosis, and tick fever. (Erlichiosis)

Ticks are a completely different type of parasite. They do not live on the dog but simply wander onto the animal in order to feed then drop off when full.

Ticks do not differentiate and will happily bite people, sheep, deer and cattle alongside dogs. They are usually only around in the summer months, but in areas of plentiful wildlife or farming environments they come in force during the warm weather, particularly when the grass gets long.

To remove a tick it is important not to squeeze its body whilst it feeds. This can cause the stomach contents and innards to be pushed into your dog's body. It is also important not to just pull, as this can leave the head under the dog's skin even if you remove the body. Be careful, because if the head is left attached this can easily lead to infection. If this happens, seek veterinary attention without delay.

Pet stores sell small hooks which can be put between the tick's body and your dog's skin for careful removal, this will safely remove the parasite completely.

I would suggest either getting a friend or vet, who has experience of how to remove ticks to help you, or watch a step by step video from YouTube.

c.) Mites

Mites are everywhere. Generally they do us no harm, yet some can cause problems for the Bichon Frisé dog, particularly the mange mite.

Mange mites burrow under the skin of the dog and cause itchiness and general hair loss. Left untreated the mange mite will affect the general health of the animal and result in eventual baldness.

The immune system of the dog is severely affected by the presence of mange mites. If not treated, the seemingly simple mange infestation will be fatal.

Any dog that is suspected of carrying mange mites should be treated by conventional veterinary medicine. The condition can be really difficult to get rid of and the course of treatment may be long and slow.

d.) Ear Mites

Ear mites cannot be seen by the human eye but are easily visible with the use of a microscope. These little mites grow and reproduce in the dog's ear and create a very smelly brown discharge. Ear mites are usually easily treated with drops.

http://www.vetstreet.com/care/chronic-otitis-chronic-ear-infection-in-dogs

3.) Other common Illnesses

Bichon Frisé health is something that every owner of the breed should be aware of. Dogs get sick sometimes, they have off days, and they are susceptible to passing bugs, just as we are.

To have a basic understanding of the way that these things affect the body of your dog, will put you in the best position to help him.

a.) Diarrhea

Diarrhea is a common occurrence and not normally one to worry too much about.

If the Bichon Frisé dog does display symptoms you can simply withhold his food for 24 hours, to allow the stomach and bowels to rest, then re-introduce it gradually.

If the following symptoms occur, then it is important to visit your veterinary surgeon as soon as possible;

- » The dog has eaten something potentially toxic such as chocolate or artificial sweetener
- » The dog is lethargic or staggering
- » The dog's gums are very pale or very dark red
- » When pinched, the back of the dogs neck does not spring back into place – this is a sign of dehydration
- » The condition does not clear up within a few days
- » The dog is passing blood

b.) Vomiting

Dogs vomit by choice, so a one off incident is usually nothing much to worry about. You will see them eating grass for instance, and then sometime later you may notice a pile of chewed up grass and mucous/stomach contents. Although eating grass doesn't always lead a dog to vomit, it may be one of the reasons you may see them vomit. It is generally thought they may vomit if they feel ill and need to empty their stomach, much the same as we may need to vomit and then feel much better afterwards.

Yet if the following circumstances are associated with vomiting, then the dog should be taken along to the veterinarian;

» The dog could have been exposed to poisons.

» The dog's airway is obstructed either alongside or as a result of vomiting.

» The dog has not long been chewing a bone or toy that could possibly be stuck in his digestive system.

If any of the previous conditions are worrying you to excess, or seem too severe to ignore, even if your concern is caused by an instinctive 'gut' feeling; this should result in a check-up with the vet.

You know your dog better than anyone else. If you are overly worried, then it is a good idea to listen to those concerns. Your Bichon Frisé dog's health may depend on your instinct at some point in your lives together.

Chapter Ten:

Keeping Your Bichon Frisé Healthy

PLEASE NOTE: The following is intended for informational purposes so that you are aware of potential diseases that can affect the Bichon Frisé. Although you will read here about a number of diseases and illnesses that a Bichon Frisé can be susceptible to, please do not assume that the Bichon Frisé is bound to contract all or any of these diseases. There are also a number of diseases not mentioned here that at some time Bichon Frisés have been reported with a low frequency. You can read veterinary guides on certain breeds and you will find, in the case of some dogs pages of diseases that at some time a particular breed, or specific dog has been affected by. Do not worry unduly about this as most dogs will get only a few mentioned and some none at all.

The most important thing you can do to keep your Bichon Frisé healthy is to provide him with a nutritious diet. Even if you give your dog a healthy diet and a safe environment, however, he may still be prone to developing certain health problems. Familiarizing yourself with the health problems to which this breed is prone will help you to identify them early on so you can provide your dog with the necessary treatment. In this chapter you will find valuable information about Bichon Frisé diseases, vaccination information, nutritional deficiencies, and pet insurance.

1.) Common Bichon Frisé Health Problems

All dogs are prone to developing certain diseases and congenital conditions can be passed from the parent dogs to the puppies. In this section you will find an overview of the various diseases to which this breed is prone. You can prepare yourself in the event that your Bichon Frisé comes down with something.

The following diseases and disorders are common for the Bichon Frisé:

» Bladder Infections/Stones

» Brachycephalic Airway Obstruction Syndrome

» Juvenile Cataracts

» Diabetes Mellitus

» Mitral Valve Disease

» Patellar Luxation

» Skin Allergies/Atopic Dermatitis

In the following pages you will receive an overview of each of these diseases including information about causes, symptoms, and treatments. The more you know about these diseases the better equipped you will be to handle them if they occur. The earlier your Bichon Frisé receives a diagnosis, the more effective treatment will be and the greater his chances of making a full recovery.

a) Bladder Infections/Stones

The Bichon Frise has a predisposition for various bladder conditions including infections and bladder stones. Bladder stones are called uroliths, so the condition which produces them is called urolithiasis. There are several types of bladder stones found in dogs but the type most common to the Bichon Frise are formed from calcium oxalate. In most cases, bladder stone formation is linked to an infection caused by bacteria that produce urease, though other bacterial infections may contribute to the condition as well.

The main cause of urolithiasis is hereditary , which is why it is important that dogs diagnosed with such a condition should never be allowed to pass this on through breeding. Both humans and dogs have a substance known as nephrocalcin in their urine which helps to inhibit the growth of bladder stones. In some dogs like the Bichon Frise, however, production of this substance is defective. A diet that is low in vitamins and minerals may contribute to bladder problems and certain metabolic diseases like Cushing's disease may increase your dog's risk for bladder stone formation.

Though bladder stones themselves may not be life-threatening, they do cause a problem when they block the urinary opening. When this happens it could lead to uremic poisoning. If the dog cannot pass the stone on his own, you may need to take him to the veterinarian to flush the stone back into the bladder. If the stone still cannot be passed, your vet may need to surgically create another urinary opening. Because the urethra is so narrow, it is difficult to surgically remove the stone unless it is first flushed back into the bladder.

In addition to obstructing the flow of urine, bladder stones can also rub the lining of the bladder which could cause bleeding and may lead to chronic bladder infections. One of the easiest ways to prevent bladder stone formation is to make sure your Bichon Frisé has a healthy diet and that he drinks plenty of water. If your dog has already had bladder stones removed, a surgical procedure called a urethrostomy may be performed to create a new opening for urine to pass through so stones do not become stuck in the urethral opening.

b) Brachycephalic Airway Obstruction Syndrome

Although this condition is not as prolific as it is with other breeds such as the Pug or Cavalier, it can still affect some Bichons. The Bichon Frisé has a fairly short face which puts this breed at risk of breathing problems and reduced exercise intolerance. This refers to a group of upper respiratory abnormalities including elongated soft palate, everted laryngeal saccules, stenotic nares, and hypoplastic trachea. Dogs with Brachycephalic Airway Obstruction Syndrome may be affected by one, several, or all of these conditions at one time.

Stenotic nares are abnormally small or narrow nostrils which restrict the flow of air through the nose. An elongated soft palate is characterized by an abnormally long soft palate (the soft tissue on the roof of the dog's mouth) which may block part of the entrance to the trachea. Hypoplastic trachea refers to a trachea (windpipe) that is abnormally narrow in diameter. Laryngeal saccules are small pouches found inside the larynx, or voice box, which get sucked into the airway during breathing. This, compounded by the restricted airflow through the nostrils, results in further obstruction of the airway.

The main symptoms of Brachycephalic Airway Obstruction Syndrome include difficulty breathing, snorting when excited, snoring whilst sleeping, reduced exercise tolerance, and coughing or gagging. These symptoms often worsen in hot or humid weather. This condition typically manifests between the ages of 1 and 4 years and both male and female Bichon Frisés seem to be affected equally by the condition.

The symptoms of Brachycephalic Airway Obstruction Syndrome worsen significantly in overweight or obese dogs, so keeping your Bichon Frisé at a healthy weight will help to prevent this condition. Dogs with mild symptoms may manage their condition with controlled exercise and limited exposure to hot, humid conditions. Certain treatments with corticosteroids or non-steroidal anti-inflammatories may be effective and oxygen therapy can be useful for short term symptom relief. The most effective long-term treatment is to surgically correct whatever anatomical abnormalities are causing the problem in your Bichon Frisé.

c) Juvenile Cataracts

This condition is typically inherited, though some cataracts are the result of another disease such as Diabetes Mellitus or Progressive Retinal Atrophy. A cataract is the darkening or clouding of the lens in the dog's eye resulting from an accumulation of proteins. There are three classifications to describe the age of onset for cataracts. Congenital (present from birth), juvenile (develop at a young age), or senile (develop later in life). There are also different levels of cataracts based on how much of the lens it covers.

Cataracts are one of the most common eye problems in dogs. If your dog develops cataracts you will notice a change in eye color, normally to a light blue, white, or gray. You may also notice inflammation inside or around the eye. Other symptoms include squinting, rubbing the eye, bumping into objects, and other signs of vision loss. Cataracts that are caused by genetic factors cannot be prevented but those caused by other diseases can be prevented by managing the primary condition.

To diagnose your Bichon Frisé with cataracts, your veterinarian will need to perform a physical exam and he may refer you to a veterinary ophthalmologist. The vet will test your dog's ability to navigate around objects and will check for foreign objects or damage to the eye. Unfortunately, surgery is the only way to permanently remove cataracts but it is not necessary in all cases. Some cataracts are mild and do not cause significant vision problems for the dog. Even if your dog's cataracts do not seem to be impeding his vision, you should still have them checked out by your veterinarian to make sure there are not further complications.

d) Diabetes Mellitus

Though the most common health problem for Bichon Frise dogs is allergies, Diabetes Mellitus is quickly catching up. Diabetes is a condition in which the pancreas doesn't produce enough insulin to regulate and process glucose from your dog's diet. This condition tends to develop in middle-aged and senior dogs as a result of several factors including weight gain, heredity, inflammation, steroidal medications, and certain viral diseases the dog has had.

Some of the most common symptoms of Diabetes in Bichon Frisés and other dogs include increased thirst, increased urination, increased appetite, and unexplained weight loss. Dogs with Diabetes may also become weak and lethargic, depressed, or easily dehydrated. In some cases Diabetes may lead to secondary complications like cataracts or vision abnormalities, seizure or convulsions, coma, and even death. Diabetes is not a condition you should take lightly if your Bichon Frisé develops it.

Dogs with Diabetes are typically diagnosed between the ages of 4 and 14 years, the average being between 5 and 10 years. Female dogs are twice as likely to develop Diabetes as male dogs, though the reason for this is unknown. Diabetes is largely diagnosed through its symptoms, though a number of diagnostic tests may be performed to confirm the diagnosis. Blood and urine tests can be performed to test for insulin insufficiency or resistance as well as hyperglycemia. Dogs with Diabetes also have an increased risk for developing urinary tract infections and kidney disease.

The most effective treatment for Diabetes is dietary modification, especially if the dog is overweight or obese. For the most part, dogs with Diabetes require a diet that is higher in fiber than usual to help reduce glucose absorption into the bloodstream. Dogs should be fed multiple small meals per day, possibly accompanied by an insulin injection. Insulin injections can be performed at home, but you should have your veterinarian show you how to properly administer the injection before you try it yourself. With dietary modification and insulin injections, Diabetes is a very manageable disease in dogs.

e) Mitral Valve Disease

Your dog's heart is divided into four chambers – top, bottom, left, and right. There are a number of valves which supply blood to the heart and keep it flowing from one chamber to another in a specific direction. Blood first travels into the right atrium then through the right ventricle into the lungs where it is oxygenated before passing into the left atrium then through the left ventricle into the rest of the body. The mitral valve of the heart is found between the left atrium and ventricle and it serves to prevent the backflow of blood into the left atrium.

This disease is caused by the degradation of the mitral valve which keeps it from closing completely. As a result, small amounts of blood leak into the left atrium which causes the heart to work harder to pump blood. Eventually, this will lead to congestive heart failure.

The cause of MVD is still unknown, but it is known that it most commonly affects older small-breed dogs. There is strong evidence to suggest that this disease is genetic which is why there is a MVD breeding protocol in place that has been of particular importance to Cavalier King Charles Spaniles. However, as MVD affects the Bichon Frisé as well as other breeds, breeders are strongly advised to follow those guidelines. We will talk more about the protocol in the breeding section. One of the first signs of MVD is a heart murmur. You can only hear this using a stethoscope and it might be slight and hard to detect. In many dogs, a heart murmur is the only sign of MVD and the dog may appear healthy otherwise. As the disease progresses, however, the murmur will get worse and the dog may show signs of heart failure.

As your dog's MVD gets worse, he will develop symptoms like coughing, lethargy, high blood pressure, reduced exercise tolerance, and fainting. Treatment options vary depending on the severity of the condition. Unfortunately there is no cure for MVD and replacement of the valve can be very expensive and risky. The typical treatment involves medications to manage the heart failure. Medications such as diuretics may help strengthen the heart and make the flow of blood easier. Sometimes switching the dog to a low-sodium diet is helpful as well.

f) Patellar Luxation

Another musculoskeletal issue, patellar luxation is a condition in which the kneecap (patella) slips out of place in the grove of the femur. This condition is fairly common in small-breed dogs including the Bichon Frisé. The most common causes of this condition are genetic malformation of the joint or trauma. In most cases, dogs start to develop clinical signs around 4 months of age. Females are about 1 ½ times more likely than males to develop this painful and progressive condition.

The symptoms of patellar luxation will vary according to the severity of the condition. In most cases, the dog only feels pain in the moment that the patella dislocates. Once it is out of position the dog may hold up its hind leg and wait for the muscles to relax so the bone slides back into the joint. Over time, the joint will become more arthritic so the dog may exhibit changes in gait or hopping. They may also become suddenly lame.

Patellar luxation can be diagnosed by x-ray and, in some cases, a fluid sample from the joint may show increased mononuclear cell activity. Your veterinarian will also perform a physical exam to test the movement of the patella. Unfortunately, medical treatments for patellar luxation are largely ineffective. Surgery is the only truly effective and long-term treatment option. In 90% of cases, surgery will cored the structure and movement of the joint and prevent the dog from becoming lame. There are two options for surgery – to deepen the groove of the femur to better hold the patella, or to permanently fasten the patella to keep it from sliding out of positon.

G) SKIN ALLERGIES/ATOPIC DERMATITIS

One of the most common health problems seen in the Bichon Frisé are skin allergies. According to the Bichon Frisé Club of America, Inc., up to 50% of Bichon Frisé are affected by skin problems. The condition of your dog's skin is like a window to his inner health. If your dog doesn't appear healthy on the outside, there is probably something wrong on the inside. Some of the most common signs of skin allergies and other skin problems include hair loss, scratching, frequent licking, rubbing the body on objects, rashes, blisters, hot spots, and lesions. Your dog may also exhibit internal symptoms like diarrhea or vomiting for certain allergies.

Like humans, dogs can be allergic to a wide variety of things including pollen, dust, mold, dander, cigarette smoke, fleas/flea products, perfumes, fabrics, and certain food ingredients. To diagnose skin allergies and other problems, your veterinarian may perform a variety of diagnostic tests. The only way to test for a food allergy, however, is to switch to an allergen-free dog food formula for 10 to 12 weeks and then to systematically introduce potential allergens to test your dog's reaction. Once you have determined the cause of the allergy you can take steps to remove it from your dog's diet.

Certain types of allergies cannot be treated by removing them from your dog's life. For example, you cannot completely prevent your dog from coming into contact with pollen or dust. Certain medications may help to manage your dog's allergy symptoms. Antihistamines like Benadryl, for example, may benefit certain dogs and supplements of fatty acids might help to improve your dog's skin and coat condition. If your dog's allergies are very severe he may require treatment with a corticosteroid medication. These medications require close monitoring by your veterinarian.

H) ADDITIONAL BICHON FRISÉ ALLERGY INFORMATION

Dog allergies can be problematic and any dog can be prone to or become allergic to anything from the dust in the home to grains in his diet.

Wheat Allergies

Wheat and grain allergy can cause so many health problems that grain free dog food is actually becoming quite a common product and many pet stores have at least one available variety, if not multiple types. What is wheat allergy though, and what problems can it cause Bichon Frisé dogs and their puppies? Wheat related health problems in dogs are actually split into three different reactions; wheat allergy, gluten allergy and gluten intolerance. Each has a slightly different reaction on the body, all with equal detriment.

In short, wheat in a dog's diet can lead to a number of different allergy related symptoms of varying severity.

Take a look;

- Itchy skin
- Open sores
- Ear infections
- Breathing problems
- Hives
- Itching of the mouth or throat
- Itchy and watery eyes
- Itchiness
- Dry skin
- Lack of coat condition and dandruff
- Loose bowel movements
- Nasal congestion
- Rash
- Skin swelling
- Vomiting

Gluten sensitivity is a reaction specific to gluten, found within wheat,

symptoms include;

- Changes in behavior
- Pain
- Muscle cramps
- Weight loss
- Fatigue

The biology behind allergic reactions, in very simple terms, is that allergy attacks the immune system of the dog. When the dog is eating a diet high in something that he is allergic to, the body has to constantly fight the introduction of the substance in the body. This leaves the dog''s immune system weakened and less able to cope with other infections and illnesses. Although wheat is one of the major factors in dog food allergy, there are many more. Ingredients in dog food range vastly dependent on the brand. Additionally they can include bright colors (to appeal to you, the dog owner) unnatural flavors and shocking chemical preservatives.

Take a look at your favorite dog food for a moment, or spend some time in the aisles of the pet store, the composition of most dog food is pretty terrifying. Long chemical names and a huge list of them are worrying to say the least.

2.) Preventing Illness -- Vaccinations

Though you may not be able to prevent your Bichon Frisé from developing certain inherited conditions if he already has a genetic predisposition, there are certain diseases you can prevent with vaccinations.

During the first few weeks of life, your Bichon Frisé puppy relies on the antibodies he receives from his mother's milk to fend off infection and illness. Once his own immune system develops however, you will be able to administer vaccines to prevent certain diseases like canine distemper, parvovirus, and rabies.

Vaccinations for dogs can be divided into two categories: core vaccines, and non-core vaccines. Core vaccines are those that every dog should receive while non-core vaccines are administered based on your dog's level of risk. Depending on where you live and how often your Bichon Frisé comes into contact with other dogs, you may not need to administer any non-core vaccines. According to the AVMA, recommended core vaccines for dogs include: distemper, canine adenovirus, canine parvovirus, and rabies. Non-core vaccines include: coronavirus, leptospirosis, Bordetella bronchiseptica, canine parainfluenza, and Borrelia burgdorferi. You will need to speak to your veterinarian about non-core vaccines to determine which ones your Bichon Frisé does and doesn't need.

The rabies vaccine can be very stressful for dogs but, unfortunately, it is necessary in the United States due to the prevalence of rabies in wild animals. Rabies has been eradicated in the U.K. so dogs living in this area will not need rabies vaccines. It is important to note, however, that some states require an annual rabies vaccine, so be sure to check with your local council regarding requirements in your area. In any case, do not administer a rabies vaccine less than one month before or after a combination vaccine.

Your veterinarian will be able to provide you with specific vaccination recommendations for your Bichon Frisé but, for reference, you will find a general vaccination schedule for dogs below.

Recommended Vaccination Schedule

Vaccinne	*Doses*	*Age*	*Booster*
Rabies	*1*	*12 weeks*	*Annually*
Distemper	*3*	*6 to 16 weeks*	*3 Years*
Parvovirus	*3*	*6 to 16 weeks*	*3 Years*
Adenovirus	*3*	*6 to 16 weeks*	*3 Years*
Para-influenza	*3*	*6 weeks, 12 to 14 weeks*	*3 Years*
Bordatella	*1*	*6 weeks*	*Annually*
Lyme Disease	*2*	*9, 13 to 14 weeks*	*Annually*
Leptospirosis	*2*	*12 and 16 weeks*	*Annually*
Canine Influenza	*2*	*6 to 8; 8 to 12 weeks*	*Annually*

Please note:

Titre testing is commonly practised to establish whether a dog that has been immunized, is in need of a booster for a specific vaccine. This is carried out by a simple laboratory blood test. If sufficient antibodies are present, then there is no need to vaccinate with that specific vaccine. Once again, please note that regular, unnecessary vaccinating,can have an adverse affect on your dogs health. It would also constitute a waste of money.

3.) Pet Insurance - Do You Need It

Many new dog owners wonder whether pet insurance is a good option or whether it is a waste of money. The truth of the matter is that it is different in different cases. Pet insurance does for your pet what health insurance does for you; it helps to mitigate your out-of-pocket costs by providing coverage for certain services. While health insurance for humans covers all kinds of health care including preventive care, disease treatment, and accident coverage, pet insurance is a little more limited. Some pet insurance plans only cover accidents while others cover illnesses. Some plans cover certain preventive care options like spay/neuter surgery or vaccinations, but generally only during a puppy's first year.

The costs for pet insurance plans vary from one company to another and from one plan to another. To give you a general idea of what a health insurance plan might cost you, consider the chart on the next page.

Pet insurance works in a very different way than health insurance when it comes to payment. With a health insurance plan you might be asked to pay a co-payment to your doctor when you visit his office but the health plan will forward the remaining payment directly to the provider. With a pet insurance plan you will be required to pay for the treatment up-front and then submit a claim to receive reimbursement for costs up to 90%. The actual amount a pet insurance plan will cover varies from one plan to another and it may depend on the deductible you select as well.

Just as you would with a health insurance plan, having a pet insurance plan requires you to pay a monthly premium. As long as you remain current with those payments, however, you are eligible to receive benefits from the plan. Again keep in mind however, that most pet insurance plans have some kind of deductible in place. A deductible is a set amount that you must pay out-of-pocket before the plan will offer reimbursement for covered services. In many cases, pet insurance plans are useful only for large expenses like cancer treatments that you normally might not be able to cover at a moment's notice. It is not, however, generally cost-effective for things like annual vet exams and vaccinations.

Estimated Cost for Pet Insurance Plans

Pet Wellness Plan	*Injury Plan (Emergency)*	*Medical Plan (Economical)*	*Major Medical Plan*
$18 to $34 per month (£11.70 to £22.10)	*$10 per month(£6.50 p/m)*	*$19 to $27 per month (£12.35 to £17.55)*	*$25 to $35 per month (£16.25 to £22.75)*
Wellness exams, Vaccinations, dental cleaning	*Injuries only (such as Poisoning and broken bones)*	*Basic coverage for accidents, emergencies and illness*	*Double benefits of Medical Plan*
3 levels (Max, plus basic)	*Max yearly benefit limit $14,000 (£9,100)*	*Max yearly benefit limit $7,000 (£4,500)*	*Max yearly benefit limit $14,000 (£9,100)*

**This information is taken from Veterinary Pet Insurance, a division of Nationwide Insurance. Prices are subject to change and are only intended to give a general idea of pricing and coverage options for pet insurance plans.

CHAPTER ELEVEN:

SHOWING YOUR BICHON FRISÉ DOG

Showing your Bichon Frisé can be a wonderful experience for both you and your pet. In training your dog, you will develop a closer relationship with him, and your dog may enjoy the experience as well.

For purebreds like the Bichon Frisé , there are many opportunities for show. One of the most prestigious dog shows in the United States is the Westminster Kennel Club Dog Show which is held in Madison Square Garden in New York City each year. This two-day show is an all-breed benched competition for conformation. In the U.K., one of the top dog shows for purebreds is Crufts. This show is open to all kinds of dogs including.

1.) Showing Bichon Frisé Dogs

As long as your Bichon Frisé is at least six months old, and AKC or UK KC registered, has no disqualifying faults, it can be shown. Spaying is a grey area, as it has generally been considered that neutered dogs cannot be shown. This is not entirely true as the KC for example, has allowed such cases. You should check this with your local Kennel Club. Winning at your fist show is very difficult. There is much to learn about the show world, and you'll need to be very prepared before you start showing your Bichon Frisé.

Bichon Frisés are one of the easiest breeds to show. You will need to attend many dog shows before both you and your Bichon Frisé give a polished performance. There are also professional dog handlers that could show your Bichon Frisé for you.

To get more information on showing, you'll need to contact your local kennel club and see if they have any handling classes or when the next show is. These are informal and casual events where all dog owners learn. These include puppies, handlers, and even judges. Losses and wins at these matches should be taken lightly. Even at a serious show, dog handlers and owners should try not to get too serious. The results are the judge's decision.

When competing at a real AKC show, every time the judge chooses your Bichon Frisé as the best male or female Bichon Frisé, it does not mean he or she is a Champion. Your dog wins up to 5 points. This depends on how many other dogs it defeats.

How To Become an AKC Champion

Your Bichon Frisé must win 15 points including 2 majors. This means defeating enough dogs to win 3 to 5 points at a time. As a competitor, you're allowed to enter any class that your Bichon Frisé is eligible for: Puppy, Novice. American Bred, Bred by Exhibitor, or Open. The Best of Breed class is for dogs that are already Champions.

This is a brief example and rules can change from time to time. Please check your countries Kennel Club for the latest rule changes and updates.

2.) What to Know Before You Show

If you plan to show your Bichon Frisé dog, there are a few things you need to know before you register. The exact rules and requirements will vary from one show to another, so pay attention to specific requirements. Before you attempt to show your Bichon Frisé, make sure your dog meets the following requirements:

» Your dog needs to be fully house-trained, and able to

hold his bladder for several hours.

» Your Bichon Frisé needs to be properly socialized, and able to get along well with both humans and other dogs.

» Your dog should have basic obedience training, and he should respond consistently to your commands and look to you for leadership.

» Your Bichon Frisé should be even-tempered, not aggressive or hyperactive in public settings.

» Your dog needs to meet the specific eligibility requirements of whatever show you are participating in. There may be certain requirements for age, for example.

» Your Bichon Frisé needs to be completely up to date on his vaccinations so there is no risk of him contracting or spreading disease among other dogs at the show.

In addition to considering these requirements, you also need to make sure that you yourself are prepared for the show.

The list below will help you to know what to bring with you on the day of the show:

» Your dog's registration information

» A dog crate and exercise pen

» Food and water bowls for your dog

» Your dog's food and treats

» Grooming supplies and grooming table

» Trash bags for cleanup

» Any medications your dog needs

» A change of clothes for yourself

» Food and water for yourself

» Paper towels or rags for cleanup

» Toys to keep your dog occupied

3.) Preparing Your Dog for Show

Your preparations for the dog show will vary according to the type of show in which you have entered. If you enter an obedience show for example, perfecting your dog's appearance may be less important than it would for a conformation

show. Before you even enter your dog into a show you should consider attending a few dog shows yourself to get a feel for it. Walk around the tent where the dogs are being prepared for show and pay close attention during the judging to learn what the judges are looking for in any given show. The more you learn before you show your own dog, the better off you will be. One of the most important things you need to do in preparation for a conformation show is to have your Bichon Frisé properly groomed so that his coat is in good condition.

Follow the steps below to groom your Bichon Frisé in preparation for show:

- The night before the show, give your Bichon Frisé a thorough brushing then trim his nails and clean his ears as well.
- Give your dog a bath and dry his coat thoroughly before brushing him again.
- Once your dog is clean, you need to keep him that way. Have him sleep in a crate that night and keep him on the leash during his morning walk.
- The day of the show, brush your Bichon Frisé's coat again.
- When you arrive at the show, keep your dog in his crate or in a fenced exercise pen so he doesn't get dirty.

When it comes time for judging, just remember that the main reason you are doing this is to have fun with your dog. Do not get too upset if your Bichon Frisé does not win. Just take notes of ways you can improve for the next show and enjoy the experience you and your dog had together that day.

Chapter Twelve:

Breeding Bichon Frisé Dogs

Breeding dogs is not something that you should do on a whim and certainly not something you should do for money. If you think that breeding your dog will be a good way to make a little extra cash you are probably wrong. You will be lucky to come out even, by the time you cover expenses to care for a pregnant female and a litter of puppies. You should only breed your Bichon Frisé if you thoroughly prepare yourself through in-depth research. You also need to be sure that you are able to provide the level of care required. You will learn the basics about breeding Bichon Frisés in this chapter.

PLEASE NOTE: The following is intended as a brief introduction of what to expect. Like many things, there are many pitfalls and problems that can be avoided with careful preparation. I would also recommend reading the following book to get an idea, and if you have not been put off, then properly research and prepare. I mention this at the end but a detailed book on the subject that you will find many forum members recommend is 'Book of the Bitch'. But for now, hopefully the following will be useful to you.

1.) Basic Breeding Information

The "MVD Protocol" was largely set up for Cavalier King Charles Spaniels. As you have probably already read, the Bichon Frisé is susceptible to a disease called Mitral Valve Disease (MVD) and it is incredibly heritable. As such, the Cavalier King Charles Spaniel Club in both the U.K. and Canada have introduced a breeding protocol to reduce the spread of this disease. According to this protocol, no Cavalier King Charles Spaniel should be bred before 2 ½ years of age and any that have been diagnosed with an MVD murmur should not be bred under 5 years of age. Dogs under 5 years of age should only be bred if their parents were free of MVD murmurs by the age of 5 years. I realise that this principally applies to CKCS's. However, if you plan to breed Bichon Frisés , I would highly recommend that you follow this protocol closely because of the aforementioned MVD link. Yet again, I realise the MVD protocol was mainly aimed at the CKCS, but I would urge anyone with a breed susceptible to MVD, to seriously consider the protocol. You can find more information at the following:

MVD Protocol:

http://cavalierhealth.org/mvdprotocol.htm

Also please do a Google search for other MVD Protocol links.

I am all in favor of breeding at least one litter of pups in order to keep the generation going of your beloved pet. If you do not wish to breed with your dog, or only intend to breed one litter, you may wish to consider the benefits to your dogs health of spaying or neutering. However, as the previous chapter on showing indicates, serious show competitors may be at a disadvantage with a dog that is spayed/neutered. So if showing dogs is something you are likely to be pursuing, please do research any show limitations relating to a spayed/neutered dog.

There is much debate about when is the ideal time to spay or neuter a dog. Traditionally between 6 months and a year was considered ideal. Incidentally, the Bichon Frisé usually receives its first heat around 6 to 11 months of age. According to 'Blue Cross' they advocate spaying or neutering before the age of 6 months, but for larger dogs this should be after the first heat. More information is available at the following https://www.bluecross.org.uk/pet-advice/neutering. However, according to the ASPCA, they suggest dogs can be spayed before 6 months of age. Spaying a female dog before her first heat is considered to significantly reduce your dog's risk for developing mammary cancer as well as ovarian and uterine cancers. To find out more, have a look at the following site; https://www.aspca.org/pet-care/general-pet-care/spayneuter-your-pet

If you are considering the option of breeding your Bichon Frisé, you will find it useful to know some facts about dog breeding in general. For example, the estrus cycle (also known as "heat") for dogs occurs twice a year; about every 6 months; though some small-breed dogs have three cycles per year. This cycle typically lasts for 14 to 21 days with the length varying from one dog to another. It can take a few years for an adult dog's cycle to become regular. Heat does not occur in any particular season, it is simply a matter of the dog's age and when she reaches breeding age.

If you plan to breed your Bichon Frisé, it will be important for you to recognize the signs of estrus. The first sign that your dog is going into heat will be the swelling of the external vulva. In some cases, your dog may excrete a bloody discharge early on but this typically does not develop until the 5th to 7th day of the cycle. As your dog's cycle progresses, the discharge will become lighter in color and more watery. By the 10th day of her cycle, the discharge will be pinkish in color.

In addition to swelling of the vulva and a bloody discharge, many female Bichon Frisés in heat will start to urinate more often than usual. You may also notice an increased appetite. Sometimes the dog will develop marking behavior, spraying urine on various objects in the home to mark her territory and to attract male dogs. A male dog can smell a female in heat from great distances, so it is very important that you keep your female Bichon Frisé indoors when she is in heat. When you take her outside, supervise her closely and never take her to a dog park or anywhere that intact male dogs may be present.

Ovulation typically occurs at the time of your dog's cycle when the vaginal discharge becomes watery. During ovulation is when your Bichon Frisé will be most fertile. If you intend to breed her, this is when you should introduce her to the male dog. Your Bichon Frisé may not be receptive to the advances of a male dog until this point in her cycle. However, she is capable of becoming pregnant at any point during estrus because sperm can survive for up to 5 days in the female's reproductive tract. If your female Bichon Frisé accidentally mates with the wrong dog you can take her to the veterinarian for a mis-mating injection. Be aware, however, that there are risks associated with this injection, so discuss it carefully with your vet.

The number of puppies your Bichon Frisé carries may vary. The average litter size is about 3 to 5 puppies. In most cases, new mothers will have smaller litters at first and then may carry more puppies until about her fourth litter when the number tapers off again.

Once your Bichon Frisé becomes pregnant, she will enter into a gestation period lasting about 63 days (9 weeks). You will not be able to detect your dog's pregnancy until the pregnancy has advanced about 3 weeks. Do not attempt to feel for the fetuses on your own because you could hurt your dog or the developing fetuses. An experienced veterinarian will be able to palpate your dog's uterus around day 28 to 32 of her pregnancy to confirm that she is indeed pregnant. It is safe to perform an ultrasound on a pregnant dog after 25 days, and by six weeks, pregnancy can be confirmed using x-rays.

2.) The Breeding Process

Again, if you are breeding Bichon Frisés, you will need to wait until your female dog is at least 2.5 years old to make sure you won't be passing on Mitral Valve Disease to the litter. This will give you plenty of time to get used to your dog's cycle.

Again, it is debatable as to the best age for a dogs first litter. It is generally considered to breed after the first or second season. The bitch should by this point be fully sexually mature You will start to recognize the signs of heat in your dog and will be able to take precautions against accidental pregnancies. An intact male dog can smell a female in heat from distances up to 3 miles (4.83 km). So do not think that just because your neighbors do not have a dog that your female will be safe. The whole season process takes approximately 3 weeks until your female is safe. Usually by the 18th day of estrus, the female is still likely to attract the attention of males, but she is unlikely to 'stand' for them. In this respect, she should be safe from any unwanted pregnancies.

Once your dogs are of proper breeding age, you can start to think about breeding. You will need to keep a record of your female dog's estrus cycle so you will know when she is most fertile; around days 11 to 15 of the cycle. During this time is when your female dog will be most receptive to breeding. So, that is when you should introduce her to the male dog. Mating behavior usually involves the male dog mounting the female from behind. The male will ejaculate his sperm into the female's reproductive tract where it will fertilize the eggs. Sometimes the two dogs become what is known as 'tied'. Effectively the male is unable to release his penis from the female vagina. So do not become distressed or try to release him in anyway. This is a perfectly natural occurrence and he will release himself in a short length of time. If the eggs are fertilized, conception occurs and the female becomes pregnant. She then enters into the gestation period which, as previously noted, lasts about 59 to 63 days.

It is also important to remember the health of the bitch prior to breeding. Obviously never consider mating her if she has some illness at the time. Even if it is a temporary skin disease that she could pass onto the pups. Ensure that any disease is clear before you breed. You should also ensure that she is neither overweight, nor underweight. Obviously you will restrict her diet if she looks too fat and feed her up if too thin.

The stud dog

The choice of a stud dog will depend on your intentions for breeding in the first place. If you are merely wishing to keep the lineage of your beloved pet, you will no doubt choose a healthy dog with a good pedigree. If you are much more serious about showing, then the pedigree and therefore stud dog, will be very specific towards a dog with a top show pedigree. As far as where to look for a suitable stud dog, I can only refer you back to the resources previously listed. If you are a member of a specific Bichon Frisé club, you will no doubt have first hand recommendations there. You can of course always check with the KC or AKC for their recommendation of top breeders. Once you find a suitable stud dog, it is likely that you will have to arrange to travel to or board your dog with them in order to facilitate a successful mating. This is obviously something you need to plan, so keeping records of the estrus cycle and therefore the optimum time to mate, is vital.

Stages of Pregnancy

Again, you must keep track of when you breed your female dog so you will know when to expect her to whelp the puppies (give birth). Once again, by the third week of pregnancy, around day 21, your veterinarian will be able to confirm whether the dog is pregnant or not. He may also be able to give you an estimate as to her litter size. Treat your pregnant female as you normally would until the fourth or fifth week of pregnancy, then you should start to increase her feeding rations proportionally with her weight gain. This has been covered in the chapter on feeding, so please refer back to that. You only need to increase your dog's diet slightly to account for her increased nutritional needs. Having said that, your dog will know how much she needs to eat, so you may be able to let her feed freely rather than rationing her food. Her feed intake is giving nutrition to her growing pups as well as herself. So in this respect, you do not need to worry about any overfeeding leading to obesity, and you certainly do not want to underfeed her. Your pregnant dog's diet should be high in protein and animal fat with plenty of calcium.

It is also around this time that your Bichon Frisé will start to look visibly pregnant. Your dog's belly will grow larger, tighter, and harder and her nipples will become especially swollen during the last week of pregnancy.

Maintaining everyday care

During her pregnancy you should carry on her normal routine of regular feeds and exercise. As she gets heavier she is unlikely to be inclined to race about as normal. However, you should ensure that she is not placed into any excitable situations which may cause her to chase after something,or play energetically with another dog. But you should make sure that she does still have daily moderate exercise. It is also a good idea to keep up with grooming her. If she has a noticeable discharge from the vulva, then it is important that you wash the area on a daily basis, with warm water. This will of course keep the area clean, but also avoid discharge deposits around the house.

It is also a good idea to weigh the mother once per week on the same day, to keep an accurate record. You will no doubt notice her getting bigger anyway, but weighing her confirms that the pregnancy and pup growth is normal. At approximately the fifth to sixth week of pregnancy, you should notice her breast get firmer.

3.) Raising Bichon Frisé Puppies

Whelping box

By the eighth week of your dog's pregnancy, in other words approximately a week before she gives birth, you will need to provide her with a whelping box. You can easily and cheaply construct a whelping box out of ply board with either metal brackets to hold the box together or four pieces of 2 inch by 2 inch timber for each corner. The height of the box should be about 15 inches high, with a front cutaway section about 6 inches high to allow the bitch easy access, but ensuring that pups cannot easily crawl out of the box. If you are not DIY inclined,you can buy relatively cheap cardboard disposable boxes. Simply do a Google search for [whelping box], and you will be presented with a number of possibilities. Whatever box you use, it should be a comfortable place lined with clean, old blankets and towels where she can give birth and care for the puppies. Remember that you may need to change the bedding from time to time if it becomes soiled, so have spare replacement blankets/towels to hand.

It is best to place this box in a quiet area where your dog will not be disturbed. If you put it somewhere that is too bright or noisy, she will just find somewhere else to whelp. She should be allowed to spend time in the box and therefore accept this as the best place to give birth. You should also make sure this room is warm and draft free.

Whelping: Other supplies

Ideally, as well as the whelping box, you should prepare yourself with important supplies to have on hand when the time comes. Hopefully you have a spare room or at the very least a corner set up especially as a nursery. I would recommend getting hold of a large cardboard box to place the various items that you may need. The following list will equip you with essential supplies for the whelping as follows:

» A heat source; this can be a heat lamp, heat pad etc (as an emergency provision hot water bottles have been known to come in very handy) This is of course to keep the mother and pups warm.

» Clean towels intended to clean up anything the mother does not.

» A couple of rolls of paper toweling will also be handy as an extra back up for cleaning.

» Newspapers will be handy if you need to change the floor covering which could get wet.

» If you have to cut the umbilical cord, a pair of blunt end scissors, surgical or white thread to tie off the end, cotton wool and antiseptic solution to dab an open wound and clean it. It will be a good idea to have a separate, sterile container to put these items in, to minimize infection. A container with surgical spirit/antiseptic solution, is also a good idea to keep items such as the scissors or a rectal thermometer to check temperatures.

» You may also wish to weigh the puppies, so a pair of suitable scales will be necessary.

Final stages of pregnancy and giving birth

During the last week of your Bichon Frisé's pregnancy you should start checking her internal temperature regularly. Using a rectal thermometer, the normal body temperature for a dog should read between 100°F and 102°F (37.7°C to 38.8°C). However, your female dog's body temperature will drop about 24 hours before contractions begin. Your dog's body temperature may drop as low as 98°F (36.6°C), so when you notice a drop in your dog's temperature you can be sure that it won't be long before the puppies arrive. Your dog will also start spending more time in the whelping box at this time. You can check on her occasionally, but do not disturb her too much or she might go elsewhere to whelp. There are other signs that her giving birth is imminent,these include; general restlessness, making nests, moving blankets about or tearing up paper you may have lying around, she may refuse food etc. It may be nothing immediately to worry about, but you can be sure she will soon go into labor.

If she goes into labor during the day, if you can, stay with her as much as possible. This is particularly important if this is her first pregnancy, as she may be anxious and need your reassurance.

When your Bichon Frisé goes into labor, you will notice obvious signs of discomfort. She may start pacing restlessly and panting, switching from one position to another without seeming to get comfortable. The early stages of labor can last for several hours with contractions occurring about 10 minutes apart. This usually occurs in waves of 3 to 5 contractions followed by a period of rest. If your Bichon Frisé has two hours of contractions without any puppies being born, take her to the vet immediately. Without a veterinary diagnosis, it is difficult to ascertain what the problem may be, but as with human pregnancies, she may need a caesarian section.

Once your Bichon Frisé starts whelping, the puppies will generally arrive every thirty minutes; following ten to thirty minutes of forceful straining from the female.

When a puppy is born, the mother will clean the puppy and bite off the umbilical cord. Not only does the licking, clean the puppy, but it helps to stimulate its breathing as well. You need to let the mother do this without you attempting to handle the puppies unless something goes wrong. If this does not happen use a clean towel to clean the puppy and make sure there is no membrane covering the puppies muzzle.

Sometimes the mother may appear to be struggling to give birth to one of the pups. Its head or its back legs may be stuck out and not going anywhere. It may be necessary for you to help her by wrapping a clean towel around the pup and gently pulling. CAUTION: Only pull when the mother is obviously pushing. Some people advise against helping the mother in this way. But if you get a pup that is being delivered legs first, there is a possibility that the umbilical cord could be wrapped around the pup and potentially strangling it.

If a puppy is not breathing

If the puppy appears to not be breathing, you will need to administer emergency first aid. Wrap the pup in a clean towel and hold his body firmly, upside down in the palms of your hand, as if you were praying, his head should be facing the ground. Now shake him back and forth but not too vigorously, in an attempt to stimulate him into action. If he fails to breath, rub his ribs. Next attempt the Heimlich maneuver as follows: Again turn the pup upside down, holding him with his back pressed to your chest. Clasp your hands on his abdomen, just below the ribs. Now give 5 thrusts, reasonably hard and sharp to the abdomen. Now look inside the mouth or if there is some mucous or object expelled, if so remove this.

PLEASE NOTE: If after a few minutes of trying a couple of procedures, I would always advise calling an emergency vet. Whilst you are waiting continue as follows.

If you still have no luck, artificial respiration will probably be your last resort. In this case, it is similar to CPR that you would administer to a human and the following would be the same for an adult dog. You will need to blow air into the pups nose and mouth. Some people prefer to use a plastic food bag with one corner cut off that you place over the pups nose/mouth, so that you are not getting his full muzzle/hair etc in your mouth.

The procedure should be as follows:

» lay the pup on his right side

» Place your hand or fingers on his ribs at the point the elbow meets the chest/ribs (this is approximately where his heart is). Some breeders will simply hold the pup firmly and simply compress the ribs. Be very careful doing this, as although this is an emergency, you do not want to break the rib cage.

» Give about 20 compressions per minute. You do this in short bursts. So 60 divided by 20 gives is 3.

» You should be able to check his pulse in the place where the elbow meets the chest or around his wrist above his front paw. You can also check the femoral artery as noted in the chapter on first aid. CPR is also discussed there.

» Repeat once more, and if there is still no pulse/breathing, give mouth to mouth resuscitation.

» So as above, either place a plastic bag with the corner removed over the pups mouth or simply cup your own mouth over the pups nose and mouth (You should make sure that you make a seal so that no air escapes, and gently blow but similar to how you would breathe out after taking a deep breath. You should now give 3 compressions and then breath air into the pup.

» Continue this sequence until hopefully the pup

starts to breathe. Dont just give up after a few minutes, at least continue until an emergency vet arrives.

Hopefully you will never have to experience this, but it is best to be aware of what to do just in case.

After the mother has given birth

After all of the puppies have been whelped, again the female will expel the rest of the placenta and then allow the puppies to nurse (feed). The bitch may attempt to eat the placenta, which is normal. It is advisable at this stage to get a veterinary check up to confirm that the bitch is healthy and to confirm all of the placentas have been expelled and not likely to cause an internal infection.

It is very important that the puppies start nursing (feeding) within 1 hour of delivery because this is when they will get the colostrum. If there is obviously a pup that has not made its way to the mothers breast soon after it is born then place it on a teat or close by. The colostrum is the first milk produced by the mother and it is loaded not only with vitamins and minerals. It also contains antibodies that will protect the puppies against illness and infection while their own immune systems are developing. After whelping, your female dog will be very hungry, so give her as much food as she will eat. As previously said, do not be alarmed if she consumes the expelled placenta as well. Please remember to count the placenta, as it is possible one or two could remain in the mother and cause an infection if not expelled. In this case she would need veterinary attention. Again do not just leave the placentas left, and if it is practical to do so, remove any remaining along with soiled newspapers.

Bichon Frisé puppies are born with their eyes and ears closed. They will also have very little fur, so they are completely dependent on their mother for warmth and care. If you suspect that the pups are not warm enough or are likely to chill over-night, consider getting hold of a heat lamp. This can be sighted above the whelping area. Care must be taken not to overheat either them or the mother. So it is perhaps best to place this at one end or a corner, therefore leaving a part of the whelping area cooler.

Growing puppies

The puppies will spend most of their day nursing and sleeping until their eyes start to open around 3 weeks of age. Between the third and sixth week after birth is when the puppies will start to become more active, playing with each other and exploring the whelping box area. The puppies will also start to grow very quickly as long as you feed the mother enough so she can produce enough milk.

Around six weeks after birth is when you should start weaning the puppies if the mother has not started already. Start to offer the puppies small amounts of puppy food soaked in water or broth to soften it. The puppies may sample a bit of the food even as they are still nursing. But they should be fully transitioned onto solid food by eight weeks of age. If you do not plan to keep the puppies yourself, it is at this time that you should start introducing the puppies to potential buyers. You should never sell a puppy that has not been fully weaned and you should carefully vet potential buyers to make sure that the puppies go to a good home.

Puppies are very impressionable during the first few months of life so you need to make sure they get as many experiences (socialization) as possible. If your puppies are not exposed to new things at a young age they will grow up to be fearful and nervous adults. Give the puppies plenty of toys to play with as their teeth start to grow in around week ten, and start playing with them yourself so they get used to being handled by humans.

This is only a very brief if not relatively detailed introduction to the breeding process. For further reading and much more information, I would highly recommend 'Book of the Bitch' by J.M. Evans & Kay White.

Summary of Breeding Information

- Age of First Heat: around 6 to 11 months
- Breeding Age: not before 2.5 years; not under 5 years unless parents were MVD murmur-free past 5 years
- Frequency: twice a year, every 6 to 7 months (could be three times a year)
- Greatest Fertility: 11 to 15 days into the cycle
- Gestation Period: 59 to 63 days
- Pregnancy Detection: possible after 21 days, best to wait 28 days before exam
- Feeding Pregnant Dogs: maintain normal diet until week 5 or 6 then slightly increase rations
- Signs of Labor: body temperature drops below normal 100° to 102°F (37.7° to 38.8°C), may be as low as 98°F (36.6°C); dog begins nesting in a dark, quiet place
- Contractions: period of 10 minutes in waves of 3 to 5 followed by a period of rest
- Whelping: puppies are born in 1/2 hour increments following 10 to 30 minutes of forceful straining
- Puppies: born with eyes and ears closed; eyes open at 3 weeks, teeth develop at 10 weeks
- Litter Size: average 3 to 5 puppies
- Weaning: start offering puppy food soaked in water

at 6 weeks; fully weaned by 8 weeks

» Socialization: start as early as possible to prevent puppies from being nervous as an adult

Chapter Thirteen:

Bichon Frisé Behavior Problems.

In this area of the book I wanted to talk about potential behavior problems that the Bichon Frisé may develop. Like people, dogs have their own specific personalities. The behavior that the Bichon Frisé displays is partly based on his nature, and mostly a result of the nurturing effect that life has had on him so far. Most canine problems can be halted before they get too severe, or even modified into manageable acts. It's important to have an understanding of behavior before trying to make any changes.

1.) Dealing with Common Behavior Problems

Once again it is not fair to generalize, as two dogs of the same breed could be either high maintenance or no trouble at all. Generally however, if your dog doesn't get enough exercise or attention he is likely to develop problem behaviors which may require professional training to correct. What you need to understand before you try to tackle any behavior problem, is that many behaviors that you might consider problematic are actually natural behaviors for your dog.

For example, chewing is a very natural way for puppies to learn about their world. They also do it to ease the pain of teething. When your puppy fulfills his need to chew by gnawing on an expensive pair of shoes, is when the behavior becomes a problem. The best way to deal with problem behaviors is not to teach your puppy to avoid the behavior altogether but to channel that behavior toward a more appropriate outlet. Below you will find tips for dealing with some of the most common behavior problems in dogs:

Chewing – The best way to keep your Bichon Frisé from chewing on things he shouldn't be chewing on is to make sure that he has plenty of toys available. Many dogs chew on things out of boredom, so ensuring that your Bichon Frisé gets enough exercise and play time, will also help to keep him from chewing on things around the house. If chewing does become a problem all you need to do is replace the item your dog is chewing on with one of his toys (swapping). Ideally you would have taken care of such items in your initial puppy proofing stage. However, we can't always be sure which he will chew and which he will ignore. You are therefore better off keeping every potential chewable item that you wish to keep intact, out of his reach.

If after this you still find your Bichon Frisé has found something you had forgotten about and is chewing on it, tell him "No" in a firm tone and take the object away. Immediately replace the object with your dog's favorite toy, then praise him when he starts chewing on it. Eventually your Bichon Frisé will learn what he is and is not allowed to chew on around the house.

Digging – Just like chewing, digging is a behavior that dogs often exhibit when they are bored. While digging is a natural behavior for dogs, it becomes problematic when your Bichon Frisé chooses to do it in the middle of your favorite flower bed, or under your fence. A simple way to deal with this problem is to provide your Bichon Frisé with a small section of the yard where he is allowed to dig. Bury a few toys or treats in the area to encourage your Bichon Frisé to dig there. If you find your Bichon Frisé digging in the yard, tell him "No" in a firm voice and lead him away from the area and into his special digging zone. Reward and praise him when he starts to dig there instead. If this becomes particularly problematic, you may simply have to fence off any such areas.

Jumping Up – Obviously the small size of the Bichon Frisé is unlikely to affect anyone but the smallest child. However, jumping up can develop into an annoyance that we should curb. We have already covered this to an extent elsewhere, but go into a bit more depth here. What many dog owners do not realize is that they actually teach their dogs to jump up on people when they come in the door or when the dog gets excited. When your Bichon Frisé is a cute and cuddly puppy it can be tempting to reward him with pets and cuddles when he crawls into your lap or jumps up at your legs. When your Bichon Frisé grows up, he expects you to react in the same way to this behavior because you have reinforced it. In order to curb this problem behavior you simply need to teach your Bichon Frisé that jumping up will not get him what he wants; your attention. You therefore ignore the behavior. Quite often as your Bichon Frisé jumps up many people instinctively hold out their hands to stop the dog. Again, this is affirming the jumping up with physical contact. The best approach is to get into the habit of turning your back, the moment he jumps up. He may try again, but will soon realise, the only way you acknowledge him is when he greets you without jumping up.

The Bichon Frisé is a very affectionate breed with family, but he can sometimes be wary around strangers unless properly socialized. For this reason, jumping up is not a behavioral problem that is particularly common with the Bichon Frisé but it is still possible. To teach your Bichon Frisé not to jump up on people, you may need to enlist the help of a friend or two. Have your friends stand outside the front door to your house and ring the doorbell. This should get your Bichon Frisé excited. After ringing the doorbell, have your friend enter the house. When your Bichon Frisé jumps up, your friend should place their hands behind their back and ignore the dog for a few seconds before turning around and leaving again.

After a few repetitions of this, have your friend give your Bichon Frisé the "Sit" command. If he complies, allow your friend to calmly pet the dog for a few seconds before leaving again. Repeat this sequence several times until your Bichon Frisé remains calm when the doorbell rings. It may take quite a few repetitions to recondition your dog against jumping up, but with consistency you can make it happen.

Whining – Similar to jumping up on you, your Bichon Frisé's whining has one goal; to get your attention. When your Bichon Frisé whines at you, stand up calmly and leave the room; go into another room and close the door. Wait for a few seconds until your Bichon Frisé stops whining, then return to the room and pet him calmly. Repeat this sequence every time your dog whines at you, and he will eventually learn that whining does not earn him your attention.

Barking – Bichon Frisés are known to be a breed that will easily bark at strangers and for other reasons. Some dogs tend to bark more than others; especially when they get excited. The easiest way to teach your dog to stop barking is actually to teach him to bark on command first.The easiest way to teach your dog to stop barking is actually to teach him to bark on command first. Again, you will need to have a friend stand outside your front door and to ring the doorbell. Get your Bichon Frisé's attention and give him the

"Speak" command. As soon as you give the command, have your friend ring the doorbell to get your dog to bark. When he does, praise him excitedly and reward him. After a few repetitions, your dog should start barking on command before the doorbell rings.

Once your dog learns to bark on command you can then teach him a "Hush" command. Give your Bichon Frisé the "Speak" command and let him bark a few times before telling him "Hush". When he stops barking, praise him and offer him a treat. Repeat this sequence several times until your Bichon Frisé gets the hang of it. Bichon Frisés are an intelligent breed that will be eager to please, so this shouldn't take too many repetitions.

So to recap, first teach the dog to bark and add a command ("Speak/Bark") to it. Next, start to reinforce the short pauses between barks and add a command ("Hush/ Quiet") to THEM. The dog will learn that the pauses are rewarded too; therefore he is rewarded for being quiet as well as to bark. But he must learn to bark on command first of all, before being taught to be quiet on command. As with any of your previous training, it is important to mark the behavior so that there is no confusion and your dog knows exactly what is expected.

Again the command word can be 'quiet' or 'be quiet'. Remember to be quick with this next bit of making him quiet. You want him to know at what point he receives a treat for being quiet. What you will hopefully get to, is the stage where you are no longer rewarding the barking, but you ARE rewarding the 'quiet'. In this way he shouldn't be so keen to bark, particularly if he knows there is no treat to follow. Of course, it is unlikely that you will stop the natural impulse for him to bark, but at least now, you should be able to quickly stop him.

The second option is better for a dog who doesn't bark very much. Once again the clicker is a great tool, but what you need to do this time, is show the dog his reward and encourage him to offer behaviors that will earn him the reward. In a way this is teasing the dog, by showing him the treat, but refusing to give it.

He will go through his repertoire in order to try and get the treat from you. Eventually he should make a sound, it may not be a bark it may not even be a growl, just a squeak. The most important thing to do is reward any sound. That sound can then be shaped into a bark by then gently withholding a reward bit by bit until the dog barks. Again, it is kind of teasing the dog, but is only necessary in these initial stages. A lot of people use this when they want to give them a treat for no apparent reason, but you wish the dog to "ask" for it. So they say something like, 'say please', whilst they are offering the treat. Obviously you only give the treat when they bark.

It may seem odd to teach your dog to bark when you wish them to stop. The point of this is that YOU are in control, telling him to either bark or stop barking. What you are doing is 'tricking' the dog into stopping with his barking, by your command/reward approach. Of course once he has mastered the 'stop barking' command, you are unlikely to need the 'start barking' command. So again, I am not suggesting that you will ever stop a dog from barking, particularly a dog with a high predisposition to bark. What you will have with this training approach however, is more control and the ability to stop him sooner.

2.) Teething

If you live with a Bichon Frisé puppy you must be prepared for teething time.

As his adult teeth begin to come through at a few months old your puppy will be desperate to chew things.

The baby teeth will probably either be swallowed or lost as the new teeth come through from underneath. It's unusual to find a puppy tooth but you might.

It is a great idea to provide the teething puppy with his own toys for this difficult time. Pet stores have a vast array of puppy teething toys, and it's worth buying your dog at least two or three of different materials.

It's important to note here that even with teething toys, your puppy may still find electrical cables an attractive alternative. As mentioned in the puppy proofing section, never allow your puppy access to any electrical cabling. If you cannot sufficiently hide these, then unplug and preferably tie these up out of harms reach. You do not need me to point out the obvious, that a chewed live cable, could result in a fatality.

3) My Dog Won't Come Back

As previously mentioned in the chapter on training even the very best behaved pet will suffer if he isn't given the opportunity for a daily walk/run. A bored dog will become depressed, destructive or even aggressive. It is thought that some dog owners refrain from giving their dogs the off lead runs they need for fear that the dog won't come back when called. It is great that an owner cares for the dogs safety, but is not really helping the dog receive vital exercise.

Please again refer back to Chapter Six, Training your Bichon Frisé dog and specifically the section of obedience training, "Come". Following the instructions and guidance there, should solve this problem.

4) Fears and Phobias

Whether they have lived in a safe home since puppy-hood, or were raised in a different environment, any dog can develop fear behaviors. Fireworks, thunder, travel, other animals and people are some examples of why your dog can become afraid.

A dog that is fearful has a very distinct body language. He will tuck his tail below his hind quarters and cower. He may try to leave the situation and look away from the frightening stimulus. It is vital that a scared dog is never cornered.

A scared or worried dog will often display calming signals. Some calming signals include yawning; a stressed dog will yawn frequently.

The yawning response is often mistaken for tiredness by an uninformed human. However, once you know what to look for, it is easily recognizable. Licking his lips; a calming signal and stress response, can take the form of a single nose lick or more. Sniffing the ground is a "leave me alone, I am invisible" plea.

Your job as the owner of a fearful dog is to neither ignore nor encourage the fear. Be aware of the situations in which your dog feels threatened and gently build him up, so that he can cope better with them. Introduce new and worrying situations gradually, and amalgamate them with rewards such as playing with a toy or receiving a treat for relaxed behavior.

A very important point is to never over sympathize with your dog as this can reinforce the fear. If he gets too much attention when he is afraid, he will either repeat the behavior for the attention, or even worse think that the stimulus is a threat which you too recognize. If he sees that the stimulus doesn't concern you, then your dog will learn that it shouldn't concern him either.

A scared dog should never be cornered or forced to accept attention. If he is, then he will become more scared, growl and possibly even snap. It is better to help him relax around people without them paying him any attention, than to push him into a negative reaction.

If the fear has an environmental cause, for instance fireworks, then it is worth trying a natural remedy to appease your dog's fear. Rescue remedy which can be bought in most chemists/drug stores, is suitable for short-term treatment of a worried dog. Your vet may also be able to suggest something to get your dog through difficult times such as on bonfire night or New Year's Eve, when there are a lot of fireworks.

5) Dogs and children

Most dogs that have been brought up with children, manage really well in a family environment. It's worth remembering that if an adult dog has never encountered children, he may find them worrying. They do, after all, move differently to adults and sound different.

If you have a dog that is worried about children, it is really important that you make your pet feel safe and secure when there are children around. And for both the dog and child's sake never take any risks. You can get children to give the dog treats, otherwise completely ignore him. He ideally needs to get used to them in his own time.

Never under any circumstance, leave a dog with a young child. There are too many cases of dogs attacking children. Dogs can be unpredictable, and children do not have the awareness that an adult has in being able to read signals that the dog needs to be left alone. Sometimes children see dogs as a toy to play with. Dogs can soon tire of a child's constant attention. It is best to teach the child that they have to respect the dog and not unnecessarily tease or harass the dog.

6) Separation Anxiety

Separation anxiety is when a dog fears being alone to the point of becoming severely stressed or distressed.

It is currently thought to be for one of an unknown number of reasons. There are two types of separation anxiety, amid other undefined reasons for the disorder. These are fear of unexpected noises or over attachment to the owner.

It is debatable and some would argue that there is no evidence that two dogs together will still not suffer separation anxiety. Having said that, dogs do become attached and when separated, display signs of distress such as pining, howling, whining etc. So I would say two dogs together do add mutual comfort. But two or more dogs can still display a type of anxiety which seems to be linked specifically with the absence of human presence from the home. As every dog is an individual, so is their experience when suffering from separation anxiety.

Some suffer greatly and become destructive to themselves and their surroundings. Others simply become sad and depressed when left alone. They leave no trace of the stress, thus leaving owners unaware that anxiety occurred at all during the dog's alone time.

The actual anxiety becomes a phobia and can become so severe that the dog develops serious stress related behaviors causing poor health, self-harm and obsessive worrying about being left alone. Dogs associate this with the behavior of their owners, and become stressed very early, in regular routines that lead to alone time.

To prevent separation anxiety in your own dog you have a number of options. The best one, if you are leaving your dog regularly, is to employ a willing neighbor or relative to periodically check in on your dog. Alternatively a doggy day caretaker or similar canine professional. This usually takes the form of a canine crèche area or similar and is wonderful for meeting the dog's mental and physical needs alongside ensuring the dog is not alone regularly for long periods of time.

A dog walker is the minimum provision that a full time, at home dog, should have when everyone is out at work all day.

Once again, the other possibility here is having two dogs. Companionship can make all the difference, whereby the dogs keep each other company and entertained. However, this doesn't always work and some dogs can still become overwhelmed with separation anxiety, resulting in the aforementioned negative behaviors.

If separation anxiety becomes a real problem, a local dog behaviorist may be the answer. They can observe your dog and create a modification program to try and alleviate his stressed reaction to being alone. This can work really well when carried out carefully.

7) Chasing Behavior

Bichon Frisés are an inquisitive breed and will want to investigate anything unusual. If let off the lead this could well involve chasing after small animals etc.

Chasing wildlife, livestock or similar animals, can be a problem with most dog breeds. Just as other animals are easy targets, so are cars, pedestrians and bikes.

Chasing behavior can also be a really dangerous game with potential fatal consequences. In the UK for example, a farmer is legally entitled to shoot a dog chasing wildlife.

The steps that we take to reform chasing behavior are similar to those which we use for social fear.

It is a gradual process of teaching the dog to stay relaxed with the trigger at a distance. You also need to Teach the dog to focus on you because you are extremely interesting. Eventually you build the dog's capacity to be near the trigger whilst he also stays relaxed and controlled.

It's important to focus on your dog's behavior carefully, and reinforce every time he looks towards you instead of at the trigger. If you can master this art alone, then your control over the behavior of your Bichon Frisé dog will improve dramatically.

8) A Local Dog Trainer

If you are having serious problems with the behavior of your dog it is vital to consult an expert.

When looking for a local trainer please ensure that they follow the guidelines that I have given here for behavior modification.

» Look for a kind trainer or behaviorist that uses careful and dog friendly methods to modify any unhelpful behavior that your dog has learned.

» Do your research and avoid anyone that wants to hurt, dominate or force train a dog. It will not work and will eventually make the behavior worse.

» Dog training and behavior is an unmodified profession therefore there are, surprisingly, a lot of self-proclaimed experts out there with no qualifications or scientific knowledge.

Chapter Fourteen:

Caring For Your Senior Bichon Frisé

When you first bring home your Bichon Frisé puppy, it's difficult to imagine that in only 12 to 15 years later, you will have to say goodbye.

1) The Senior Bichon Frisé

All dog breeds approach old age in the same way, but at different times, depending on their breed and size. Smaller dog breeds tend to live longer. Some dog breeds are still jumping agility courses at 13 years of age. Again, depending on the size, many other purebred dogs may only live to 8 or 9 years of age. Keep in mind that good health begins during puppy-hood and lasts a lifetime.

Your Bichon Frisé has most likely been your best friend for life. You've both shared so many experiences. Your Bichon Frisé will depend on you throughout his life. You've made a commitment to take care of him from puppy-hood to the end. Keep in mind that your Bichon Frisé will change as he ages. His body and natural exuberance may sometimes allow you to forget his age. Then one day you'll look into your Bichon Frisé's eyes and notice his silvery face, and stiffened gait. He'll most likely sleep longer, and may be less eager to play. As your Bichon Frisé nears his ten or twelve year mark, he may start slowing down on his walks. Getting your Bichon Frisé to live comfortably during his senior years need not be a challenge, but needs to be well-prepared for.

a) Caring for your Senior Bichon Frisé

Most Bichon Frisés will show signs of slowing down by graying of the coat and usually around the eyes and face. They will have a flaky coat, loss of hair, slowness of gait and enjoying the family couch more than usual. Activities like running, jumping, eating and retrieving will become more difficult for him. That said, other activities like sleeping, barking, and a repetition of habits may increase. Your Bichon Frisé will want to spend more time with you, and will go to the front door more often when you are leaving.

As your Bichon Frisé ages, he'll need certain therapeutic and medical preventative strategies. Your veterinarian will advise you on special nutritional counseling, veterinary visits and screening sessions for your senior Bichon Frisé. A senior-care Bichon Frisé program will include all of these.

Veterinarians will determine your Bichon Frisé's health by doing blood smears for a complete blood count, which will include the following:

» Serum chemistry profile with electrolytes

» Urinalysis

» Blood pressure check

» Electrocardiogram

» Ocular tonometry (pressure of the eyeball)

» Dental prophylaxis

Extensive screenings for senior Bichon Frisés is recommended well before dog owners begin to see the symptoms of aging, such as slower movement and disinterest in play and other activities.

By following this preventative program, you will not only increase your Bichon Frisé's chance of a longer life, but you'll also make his life so much more comfortable. There will be so many physical changes like loss of sight through cataracts, arthritis, kidney problems, liver failure, and other possible degenerative diseases. Adding to that you may notice some behavioral changes related to aging. Bichon Frisés suffering from hearing and eyesight loss, dental pain or arthritis may often become aggressive because of the constant pain that they have to live with. Bichon Frisés that are near deaf or blind may also be startled more easily at the slightest environmental changes. Do your best not to move furniture around in your home, and to keep things as they are, as this can be unsettling for them. Senior Bichon Frisés suffering from senility may do many unusual things, and will often become impatient.

b) House Soiling Accidents

These are associated with loss of bladder control, kidney problems, loss of mobility, loss of sphincter control, physiological brain changes, and reaction to new medications. Your older Bichon Frisé will need more support than ever, especially doing his toilet business.

Avoid feeding your senior Bichon Frisé too many unhealthy treats. Obesity is a common problem in older dogs as they naturally become less active. Additional weight will put extra stress on his joints and his body's vital organs. Some breeders suggest supplementing meals with high fiber foods that are also low in calories. You can also ask your veterinarian for a special prescription diet that best suits the needs of your senior Bichon Frisé.

c) Every Day Tips

» Never punish or use harsh tones against your senior Bichon Frisé for anything at all.

» Protect your Bichon Frisé, and foresee his reactions to any environmental changes.

» Pay special attention to his immediate needs such as going to the toilet, pain levels and eating habits.

» Visit your veterinarian often and work together on providing your senior Bichon Frisé with the best of care.

» Keep your Bichon Frisé company. Your Bichon Frisé does not understand why he's losing his sight or hearing. The world may seem to be a strange place to him right now. Comfort him frequently, and try to leave a family member with him when you go out. Your Bichon Frisé will appreciate the companionship.

» Older Bichon Frisés may not be able to wait until morning to go outdoors. Provide him with alternatives such as puppy pads or spread out newspaper, to relieve himself on during the night/early hours.

Be consistent with your schedule and do not change the way things are in your home. Doors that have always remained open should stay that way. Leave his favorite couch in the same place.

d) Keeping a Diary

You may wish to keep a diary to note the day-to-day record of how your Bichon Frisé is feeling and whether he is eating, drinking and walking. As a dog owner you are able to observe all your Bichon Frisé's activities, and record how your Bichon Frisé feels and behaves.

e) Check list of questions about your aging Bichon Frisés condition

» Is your Bichon Frisé still happy to see you and how does he respond? Is it with his usual wag or does he seem to be less responsive than normal?

» Record his respiratory rate each evening when your Bichon Frisé is resting peacefully. Record the breaths taken per minute.

» Does he still come to you when called? What is his reaction to your being there? Record the levels of anxiety and pain. When he wags his tail or walks to you.

» Can your Bichon Frisé still walk? Does he still get up and come to you? How far can he walk until he tires?

» How much pain does your Bichon Frisé seem to have? Does he have many episodes of pain? Does he yelp when handled or display signs of aggression when handled?

» Does your Bichon Frisé eat if presented with his favorite foods? Does your Bichon Frisé pick at his food or refuse to try some?

» Does your Bichon Frisé still drink fluids? How much fluid per day/week. Dog owners can measure fluid intake per day.

» Is your Bichon Frisé defecating, and how often does this occur? Are all his feces normal?

» Is any disease/illness worsening or improving?

» Weigh your Bichon Frisé every day or every week. If he is losing weight, how much weight is your Bichon

Frisé losing each week or month? Weight is an important indicator of health.

f) Is There An Emergency Health Deterioration Stage

Your Bichon Frisé could suffer from an acute situation that is related to their condition. These chronic or acute episodes of disease related deterioration require immediate veterinary treatment. Some internal cancers will present themselves with hemorrhaging and states of severe shock and collapse. Congestive heart failure results in distressed breathing and pulmonary edema. Bichon Frisés with renal failure, for example, will start vomiting blood and go into shock.

g) Symptoms of Pain in Your Senior or Terminally Ill Bichon Frisé

It is always devastating when medical treatment does not work. But it's also important to think about the potential suffering of your Bichon Frisé and how he was before the illness or injury. So as to determine whether your Bichon Frisé is in pain or not, veterinarians and most importantly Bichon Frisé owners need to have a way to determine a Bichon Frisés' pain and pain threshold.

Typical symptoms are as follows:

» Whimpering, whining and yelping when touched.

» Your Bichon Frisé yelps when he tries to get from point A to point B.

» Your Bichon Frisé is often depressed, and does not want to interact with other animals or people in the household.

» Sleeplessness, listlessness and hiding under the bed or in dark places.

» Your Bichon Frisé is squinting which is typical for head and eye pain in animals. Some dogs will squint both eyes when experiencing head pain.

» Your Bichon Frisé has an elevated heart rate.

» Your Bichon Frisé injures himself by attacking or injuring the pain inflicted area.

» Chattering of the teeth is suggestive of mouth pain and dental pain, but is also indicative of shock, overall trauma and pain throughout the body.

» Your Bichon Frisé is drooling excessively. This is suggestive of pain and trauma.

2) Time To Say Goodbye!

If you are lucky, those 12 to 15 years or so, are what you get; a number of years that feel so very short. Nonetheless, mercifully, although we are aware of the unfair discrepancy between our dogs' lifespan and ours, we always somehow manage to push aside this fact; that is, until we are facing the very end with our dogs.

The heartbreaking decision to "put down" or euthanize your dog is an issue frequently faced by pet parents and veterinarians. You will never be prepared for this day. Putting your Bichon Frisé to sleep is an extremely difficult and upsetting decision that you will need to make with your veterinarian. As a Bichon Frisé owner, you will usually be making this decision when your Bichon Frisé goes through one or more life-threatening symptoms that will force you to seek veterinary help immediately.

If the prognosis indicates that the end is near and that your Bichon Frisé is in great pain, euthanasia may be the right choice. It is a difficult and heartbreaking decision for any dog lover. But if the dog is suffering then it is cruel to prolong their agony.

3) What is Euthanasia

Just the thought of euthanasia or putting our Bichon Frisé to sleep is enough to make anyone cringe. There are varying opinions about this final decision. What are the rights and wrongs? Are we actually helping our dogs or being selfish? Do we have the right to end a life?

Euthanasia refers to the planned and painless death of a dog that is suffering from a painful condition, or who is old and cannot walk, cannot see or unable to control his bodily functions. It is usually done with an overdose of an anesthetic.

The process of euthanasia takes a matter of seconds. Once the injection takes place it quickly enters the blood stream and the dog goes to sleep. The overdose suppresses the heart and brain function, in turn causing an instant loss of consciousness and therefore, pain. The animal dies peacefully while asleep.

The difficult decision to euthanize your senior or sick Bichon Frisé is never an easy one, and one that may take a while for you to come to terms with. This time is usually stressful for you and your family. If this is a first time in dealing with the death of a loved one, you'll need your family by you.

4) What happens afterwards

I know many vets who will give the owner of their beloved pet, the option to take them away and bury them in a quiet area of their garden. This may well be a favorite spot that their Bichon Frisé frequented. You are generally advised to dig a hole deep enough to avoid the problem of foxes or similar predators, digging the body up.

If your Bichon Frisé is buried in a pet cemetery, or in your yard, it's also a good idea to plant a special tree or stone over the site. A few dog owners prefer to leave their deceased dogs at the veterinary clinic. Today, many pet parents opt for individual cremation. Your veterinarian can help to arrange the cremation service, and will also be able to advise you on where to find a suitable pet cemetery.

Most dog owners have given a considerable amount of thought as to what makes a fitting tribute to honour our dogs. There's no better way to do this than by commissioning a great portrait of your Bichon Frisé. This simple act will keep your memories alive and bring you happiness when time has healed your pain. After spending nearly a decade together sharing life's most special moments, you'll be able to recall your Bichon Frisé's most happy, crazy and sometimes most peaceful moments with a portrait. Professional studio photos are also a great alternative to this. After some time you may miss not having your friend around. You may perhaps wish to give a loving home to another Bichon Frisé.

Obviously you are not attempting to replace your friend, but have such love for the breed that this seems a natural thing to consider. Many dog owners breed one litter of pups for this very reason. In that way they keep the generation of their beloved dogs intact.

Adopting a Bichon Frisé from a rescue is another excellent option. Perhaps you may want to adopt a different breed so that you'll not make comparisons. Most dog owners will usually choose the same breed because they understand and love the temperament. Perhaps the best thing that you can do for yourself as well as your departed Bichon Frisé will be to adopt another Bichon Frisé.

" If there are no dogs in heaven, then when I die I want to go where they went."

-Will Rogers

Chapter Fifteen:

Websites, Miscellaneous Resources & Conclusion

Caring for a dog can be challenging so you can probably use all the help you can get. In this chapter you will find a collection of useful resources to help you be the best Bichon Frisé owner that you can be. Here you will find links to suppliers for Bichon Frisé food, crates, dog beds, toys, accessories and more. You will also find links to additional resources about the Bichon Frisé Breed.

Please note: The following are a few suggestions for on-line suppliers in both the USA and the UK. It is intended to give you a good start, locating various supplies that you will no doubt need. It is not intended as a definitive list, nor is the author in anyway recommending or endorsing any of these. They are considered to be good suppliers, but again it is up to you to do your own research and decide who you wish to deal with.

I would also suggest doing a Google search for additional suppliers. You will also no doubt have local suppliers in your area. Also please be aware that general pet stores usually have items and feed, so please do check those also. Once you gain experience, you will no doubt have your own favorites. I would always urge you to shop around, and not necessarily go for the cheapest, particularly where feed is concerned.

Please also note that at the time of press, the following web links were working. However, from time to time, pages get changed, deleted or a supplier goes out of business. If you find these do not work, please go to the route .com or .co.uk web address. Again, the author takes no responsibility for the availability of any of these, when you the reader comes to access them.

1.) Food for Bichon Frisé Dogs

Providing your Bichon Frisé with a healthy diet is the key to maintaining good health. In this section you will find a collection of relevant websites for Bichon Frisé food.

United States Links:

Nutro Natural Choice Small Breed Dog Food.

http://www.nutro.com/natural-dog-food/nutro/dry/small-breed-adult-chicken-whole-brown-rice-oatmeal-recipe.aspx

Blue Buffalo Life Protection Formula – Small Breed.

http://bluebuffalo.com/natural-dog-food/healthy-holistic-blue-life-protection-formula/dry-food/lpf-small-breed-adult-chicken-and-brown-rice-recipe/

Earthborn Holistic – Small Breed Natural Dog Food.

http://www.earthbornholistic-petfood.com/us/dog_formulas/small_breed/

1-800-PetMeds – Small Breed Dog Foods.

http://www.1800petmeds.com/Small+Breed+Dog+Food-cat240005.html

United Kingdom Links:

Eukanuba – Small Breed Lamb Dog Food Formula.

http://www.eukanuba.co.uk/products/for-dogs/eukanuba-adult-dry-dog-food-for-small-_a_-medium-

breed-lamb-_a_-rice

Canagan Free-Run Chicken – Small Breed Dogs.
https://www.canagan.co.uk/small-breed-chicken.html

Iams ProActive Health – Adult Small and Medium Breed.
http://www.iams.co.uk/dog-food/iams-proactive-health-adult-small-medium-breed

More Pet Foods – Small Breed Adult.
http://www.morepetfoods.co.uk/more-small-breed-adult-dog-food-2kg

"Feeding Small Breed Dogs."
http://www.purina.co.uk/content/your-dog/feeding-your-dog/the-right-food-for-your-dog/feeding-small-breed-dogs

2.) Crates and Beds for Bichon Frisé Dogs

Your Bichon Frisé's crate is the place where he can retreat if he wants a nap or to take a break. In this section you will find a collection of relevant websites for dog crates and beds.

United States Links:

"Crates, Carriers, and Pens." Drs. Foster and Smith.
http://www.drsfostersmith.com/dog-supplies/dog-cages-crates-carriers-pens/ps/c/3307/10627

"Dog Beds." Cabela's. http://www.cabelas.com/

"Crates." PetSupplies.com. http://www.petsupplies.com

http://www.petsupplies.com/dog-supplies/crates/9113/

"Crates, Gates and Containment." PetsMart. http://www.petsmart.com

http://www.petsmart.com/dog/crates-gates-containment/cat-36-catid-100013

Dog Beds – Orvis.com.
http://www.orvis.com/dog-beds

"Dog Beds, Crates and Gear." Chewy.com.
http://www.chewy.com/dog/crates-kennels-369

"Dog Beds and Mats." In the Company of Dogs.
http://www.inthecompanyofdogs.com/ShopCategory.aspx?ID=17,470

"Dog Carriers." PetSmart.
http://www.petsmart.com/dog/Carriers/cat-36-catid-100085

United Kingdom Links:

"Orvis Dog Beds." Orvis United Kingdom.

http://www.orvis.co.uk/dog-beds#close

"Dog Crates." PetPlanet.co.uk. http://www.petplanet.co.uk

http://www.petplanet.co.uk/category.asp?dept_id=771

"Dog Crates and Kennels." Amazon.co.uk.

http://www.amazon.co.uk

Please search for dog crates and kennels

"Dog Crates." RSPCA.org.uk. http://www.rspca.org.uk

http://www.rspca.org.uk/adviceandwelfare/pets/dogs/environment/crates

"Dog Beds and Bedding." Pet-Supermarket.co.uk. http://www.pet-supermarket.co.uk

https://www.pet-supermarket.co.uk/Dog/Dog-Beds-Bedding/c/PSGB00051

3.) Toys and Accessories for Bichon Frisés

Having the right toys and accessories for your Bichon Frisé is very important. In this section you will find a collection of relevant websites for Bichon Frisé toys and accessories.

United States Links:

"Interactive Dog Toys." Petco. http://www.petco.com

http://www.petco.com/N_22_101/Dog-Toys.aspx

"Dog Toys." Chewy.com. http://www.chewy.com

http://www.chewy.com/dog/toys-315

"Bowls & Feeders." PetSmart. https://www.petsmart.com

https://www.petsmart.com/dog/bowls-feeders/cat-36-catid-100010

"Dog Toys." Drs. Foster and Smith. http://www.drsfostersmith.com

http://www.drsfostersmith.com/dog-supplies/dog-toys/ps/c/3307/3

PetEdge Dog Grooming Supplies.

https://www.petedge.com/zpetedgemain/contentmanagement/home.jsf?wec-appid=PEDM_WEBSHOP_TR&wec-locale=en_US&wd=x

"Interactive Dog Toys." Petco

http://www.petco.com/N_22_101/Dog-Toys.aspx

"Collars, Harnesses and Leashes." PetSmart.

http://www.petsmart.com/dog/collars-harnesses-leashes/cat-

36-catid-100012

"Dog Grooming Supplies." Drs. Foster and Smith.

http://www.drsfostersmith.com/dog-supplies/dog-grooming/ps/c/3307/5

United Kingdom Links:

"Dog Toys." PetPlanet.co.uk. http://www.petplanet.co.uk

http://www.petplanet.co.uk/dept.asp?dept_id=16

"Dog Feeding and Watering Supplies." Amazon.co.uk.

http://www.amazon.co.uk

Please search for dog feeding and watering

"Dog Toys." VetUK. http://www.vetuk.co.uk

http://www.vetuk.co.uk/dog-toys-c-439

"Toys." Battersea Dogs & Cats Home.

http://www.battersea.org.uk

Please search for toys on their site

"Dog Bowls & Feeders." Pet-Supermarket.co.uk. http://www.pet-supermarket.co.uk

https://www.pet-supermarket.co.uk/Dog-Bowls-and-Feeders/c/PSGB00064

Pets at Play: 10 Best Dog Toys." The Independent.

http://www.independent.co.uk/extras/indybest/house-garden/crufts-2014-indestructible-dog-toys-9170885.html

"Dog Toys." Pet-Supermarket

http://www.pet-supermarket.co.uk/Category/Dog_Supplies-Dog_Toys

"Dog Grooming Supplies." PetZone.

http://www.petzone.co.uk/dog/dog-grooming.html

Friendly Dog Collars.

http://www.friendlydogcollars.com/

"Dog Grooming Supplies." Pet-Supermarket.

https://www.pet-supermarket.co.uk/Dog/Dog-Grooming/c/PSGB00058

4.) General Dog Care Information

The key to being the best Bichon Frisé owner you can be, is to learn everything there is to know about dog ownership. In this section you will find a collection of relevant websites about various aspects of dog ownership.

United States Links:

"Dog Care." ASPCA.org.

https:// www.aspca.org/ pet-care/ dog-care

"Pet Care Center: Dog." PetMD.

http:// www.petmd.com/ dog/ petcare

"Dog Care and Behavior Tips." The Humane Society of the United States.

http:// www.humanesociety. org/ animals/ dogs/ tips/? referrer = https:// www.google.com/

"Dog Diet and Nutrition." WebMD.

http:// pets.webmd.com/ dogs/ guide/ diet-nutrition

United Kingdom Links:

"Dogs – Dog Welfare." RSP-CA.org.uk.

http:// www.rspca.org.uk/ advice-andwelfare/ pets/ dogs

"General Advice About Caring for Your New Puppy or Dog." The Kennel Club.

http:// www.thekennelclub.org. uk/ getting-a-dog-or-puppy/ general-advice-about-caring-for-your-new-puppy-or-dog/

"Caring for the Older Dog." Blue Cross for Pets.

http:// www.bluecross.org.uk/ pet-advice/ caring-older-dog

"Caring for Dogs and Puppies." Battersea Dogs & Cats Home.

http:// www.battersea.org. uk/ WEBShopItem? pid = 01tb-0000003JjxKAAS

Miscellaneous Resources

Organisations U.S.A

Bichon Frisé Club of America

http://bichon.org/

Please also search Google for regional clubs in your area.

Organisations UK

The Bichon Frisé Club of Great Britain

http://www.bichonfriseclubofgb.com/

There will also be a number of regional clubs which you can quickly locate on Google.

Resources; Further Reading and Information

AKC Gazette:

akc.org/pubs/gazette/

Dog World:

dogworld.co.uk

http://www.dogsnaturallymagazine.com/

http://www.yourdog.co.uk/Dog-Breeds/bichon-frise-dog-breed-profile.html

Animal Protection Organizations To Support

Humane Society International (HSI): hsi.org
http://www.humanesociety.org/

SPCA International
spcai.org

International Animal Rescue:
internationalanimalrescue.org

International Fund For Animal Rescue (IFAW) :
ifaw.org

Soi Dog Rescue:
soidog.org/en/about-soi-dog/
PETA:
http://www.peta.org/international/

Other Links

http://bichonfriseusa.com/

http://www.dogbreedhealth.com/bichon-frise/

http://www.bichonfrisehealthuk.org/

http://www.dailymail.co.uk/health/article-2013838/Allergy-free-pets-Dont-waste-money-hypoallergenic-dog-urge-experts.html

"Bichon Frisé." American Kennel Club.
http://www.akc.org/dog-breeds/bichon-frise/

"Bichon Frisé." Kennel Club (UK).

http://www.thekennelclub.org.uk/services/public/breed/standard.aspx?id=6148

"Bichon Frisé." DogTime.com.
http://dogtime.com/dog-breeds/bichon-frise

Animal Planet.
http://www.animalplanet.com/search/?q=bichon+frise

"Diabetes in Dogs (Type 1 and Type 2)." PetWave.
http://www.petwave.com/Dogs/Health/Diabetes.aspx

"Grooming Tips." The Bichon Frisé Club of America, Inc.
http://bichon.org/grooming-tips/

Jones, Anne. "The Health of the Bichon Frisé." Bichon Frisé Club of America, Inc.
http://www.bichonhealth.org/

http://www.bichonhealth.org/HealthInfo/HealthIssue.htm

Kennel Club UK: Bichon Frise and general health
http://www.thekennelclub.org.uk/services/public/breed/health.aspx?id=6148

http://www.thekennelclub.org.uk/media/451962/breeding_health.pdf
http://www.thekennelclub.org.uk/health/

"Estrus Cycle in Dogs." VCA Animal Hospitals.

http://www.vcahospitals.com/main/pet-health-information/article/animal-health/estrus-cycles-in-dogs/5778

"How Will Spaying Change my Dog?" ASPCA.

https://www.aspca.org/pet-care/virtual-pet-behaviorist/dog-behavior/how-will-spaying-change-my-dog

"Plans and Coverage." Veterinary Pet Insurance.

http://www.petinsurance.com/plans-and-coverage.aspx

"Plants Potentially Poisonous to Pets." Humane Society.

http://www.humanesociety.org/assets/pdfs/pets/poisonous_plants.pdf

"Vaccination Schedules for Dogs and Puppies." PetEducation.com.

http://www.peteducation.com/article.cfm?c=2+2115&aid=950

"Basic Calorie Calculator." PetMD

http://www.petmd.com/blogs/nutritionnuggets/jcoates/2013/aug/how-many-calories-does-dog-need-30849

Alternatively search Google for [basic calorie calculator]

"Nutrients Your Dog Needs." ASPCA.

https://www.aspca.org/pet-care/dog-care/nutrients-your-dog-needs

"What Causes Nutrient Deficiencies in Dogs?" Dog-Nutrition-Naturally.com.

http://www.dog-nutrition-naturally.com/nutrient-deficiencies.html

"Your Dog's Nutritional Needs." National Research Council.

http://dels.nas.edu/resources/static-assets/banr/miscellaneous/dog_nutrition_final_fix.pdf

"The Dog Food Project." http://www.dogfoodproject.com/index.php?page=main

"Canine Terminology."

https://www.thekennelclub.org.uk/media/471961/glos_of_terms_rtf.pdf

http://www.akc.org/about/glossary/

http://www.gopetsamerica.com/dogs/terminology.aspx

"Crate Training." The Humane Society of the United States

http://www.humanesociety.org/animals/dogs/tips/crate_training.html?referrer=https://www.google.com/

"Getting Started Showing Your Dog." AKC.org.

http://www.akc.org/events/conformation-dog-shows/getting-started-showing/

"How to Choose an Experienced Dog Breeder." PetMD.

http://www.petmd.com/dog/care/evr_dg_breeders

"How to Find a Responsible Dog Breeder." The Humane Society of the United States.

http://www.humanesociety.org/issues/puppy_mills/tips/finding_responsible_dog_breeder.html?referrer=https://www.google.com/

Additional Links

http://cani-cross.co.uk

http://www.canicrossusa.com

http://www.agilitynet.com

http://www.flyball.org

http://www.flyball.org.uk

https://apdt.com/

http://drsophiayin.com

http://www.ahvma.org

http://www.bahvs.com/

International Association of Animal Massage & Bodywork: also Association of Water canine Therapy

http://www.iaamb.org/preferred-educational-providers.php

Tellington TTouch UK:

http://ttouchtteam.co.uk/

Forums

http://www.dogforum.com/
http://www.petforums.co.uk/
http://www.petforums.co.uk/threads/bichon-frise-health-concerns.250662/

http://www.eurobichons.com/

Arknaturals

https://arknaturals.com/

Doggie doors are also a great way to promote healthy Toilet habits. These are a great way for your dog to come and go as he pleases. Be aware that other pets and animals could enter back into your house. You would also not want to leave these open whilst you are away from the house, in case of intruders having easy access to your property. The following are a few examples, but again research as many possibilities as you can.

https://www.petdoors.com/

http://store.intl.petsafe.net/en-gb/doors/large-dog

Conclusion

Hopefully you have read this far and have found the contents useful, informative and inspiring. There is a lot to consider when buying any dog, and consequently to appreciate their needs. Hopefully this book reflects that. For the most part, dogs that are properly looked after with love, care and respect, will repay you with unconditional love and devotion, many times over. The intention of the book was not to overwhelm you the reader and put you off committing to being the guardian of this fantastic Bichon Frisé breed. The intention was simply to give you as broad an appreciation as possible, so that you are fully prepared and equipped to properly look after and appreciate your new friend. As you will realize, having read the various chapters, keeping a dog happy does not necessarily come without its problems. However, with correct awareness and training, many potential problems can be avoided. The health and welfare of your new Bichon Frisé should go without saying, so please do everything you can to provide healthy food and a safe warm environment. In essence, it doesn't take a lot to keep your dog happy and healthy.

At the very least you should be providing the following:

(i) A warm safe habitat. (ii) Healthy food and fresh water, daily. (iii) Routine health procedures such as worming, flea treatment and veterinary check-ups. (iv) Basic training and regular daily exercise. (v) As much love and attention as you can provide.

Please remember that physical health can be counteracted by lack of mental stimulation. Whilst you can groom a dog all day long, thus pampering and giving him attention, if he doesn't get a free run, then he won't be truly happy. Secondly it is vital to embrace scientific finding on the way your dog learns. In summary; Dominance dog training is a myth that bypasses scientific findings on actual dog behavior. A dog learns from his environment and the attention, response that his own behavior provokes. This is positive reinforcement in action. Punishment after a behavior will not make the behavior go away, because each time a behavior is carried out it is forming a habit. It is possible to mask an unhelpful behavior but it makes the dog feel bad and actually makes the behavior worse. True behavior modification takes time and is carried out with kindness. The only true form of punishment to use is taking away attention when a behavior is problematic. This is called negative punishment and finally, our dogs do talk to us and we need to respect this by learning a little of their language. Thank you for reading and allowing me to explain a little of what I know about your dog's mind and needs.

INDEX

24244618R00101

Printed in Great Britain
by Amazon